The
CAMERA SMART
Actor

The CAMERA SMART *Actor*

Richard Brestoff

A Career Resource Book

SK

A Smith and Kraus Book

A Smith and Kraus Book
Published by Smith and Kraus, Inc.
One Main Street PO Box 127 Lyme, NH 03768

Manufactured in the United States of America

First Edition: October 1994
10 9 8 7 6 5 4 3 2 1

The Introduction: *A Better Way* first appeared in the April 1993 edition of Dramatics Magazine, Vol. 64#8 as a feature entitled "*The Actor Unprepared.*" © 1993 by Educational Theater Association, 3368 Central Parkway, Cincinnati, OH 45225.

Library of Congress Cataloguing-in-Publication Data

Brestoff, Richard.
    The camera smart screen actor / Richard Brestoff.
        p. cm. -- (A career resource book)
    Includes bibliographical references (p. -) and index.
    ISBN 1-880399-76-8 : $14.95
    1. Motion picture acting. I. Title. II. Series.

    PN1995.9.A26B74   1994
    791.43'028--dc20
                                    94-34487
                                         CIP

This book is dedicated to
my wife, Deborah,
my daughter, Jenny,
and to the voice in my head,
Mr. Peter Kass.

Special thanks to Stephanie Ogle and her wonderful store *Cinema Books* in Seattle, to Pat and Jim French, Michael Korolenko, Mark Elliott, Nate Long, Adele Becker, Dr. Barry Witham and Jacqueline Mok for their belief. To Mary Alice Kier and Anna Cottle of *Cine/Lit Representation* for having such faith in this book and for their perseverance in finding the right publisher. To Marisa Smith, Eric Kraus, Julia Hill and everyone at *Smith and Kraus, Inc.,* the right publishers, for their dedication and hard work, and to Olympia Dukakis for her kind words and insight. Finally, I wish to thank all my teachers and students from whom I continue to learn.

Biography

RICHARD BRESTOFF has spent 18 years of his working life in front of the camera. He has acted in over a dozen feature films, including *My Favorite Year, The Entity*, and *Car Wash*, and more than 30 Network television shows, including *Northern Exposure, thirtysomething, Night Court, Twilight Zone, Hill Street Blues* and had a reoccurring role on *Tour of Duty*. After graduating Phi Beta Kappa from University of California at Berkeley, he went on to receive his Masters of Fine Arts degree in acting from New York University's School of the Arts. In addition to his film expertise, Mr. Brestoff's experience in theater and radio drama includes the 1976 Broadway production of *Hamlet* and a part with the KIRO Radio Mystery Theater in Seattle. He is a 3 time Prime time Emmy award judge, a member of the Performer's branch of the Academy of Television Arts and Sciences and currently lives and teaches in the Seattle area. He can be reached on his E-Mail account on America On-Line at RBrestoff@AOL.com.

Preface

In 1975, I graduated from New York University's School of the Arts with a Master of Fine Arts degree in my hand, and three rigorous years of actor training behind me. I was soon lucky enough to land a part in a PBS television drama. I was nervous, but said to myself, I'm ready, I'm trained.

I was pretty keyed up when I arrived at the location for my first day of shooting. But when I got on the set, I settled down to the task at hand. I put everything into the shot, and was quite spent when the director finally said cut and print. Satisfied that I'd survived my first day of camera work, I went back to my trailer and changed into my street clothes.

A few moments later, the second assistant director knocked at my door. When I opened it, he stared at me, looking stricken. I asked him what was wrong. After a long silence, he asked me what I was doing in my street clothes. I said I was going home. Now he looked worse and asked me what I was talking about. I explained to him that I'd just finished today's scheduled scene so I was leaving. I picked up my keys. Wait, he said. We've only shot the master. What is a "master," I asked. Slowly he came up the steps and sat on a tiny seat across from me. He asked me if

I'd ever worked before. Yes, I said, in the theater, but this was my first camera job. Taking a deep breath, he told me he didn't have a lot of time to explain because they were ready for me on the set, but, he said hurriedly, in film, scenes are shot over and over again from different angles and later edited together. You mean I have to do it again? I asked. All day, he replied, adding that he'd tell them I'd be ready in a few minutes.

The rest of the day was one of the worst of my life. I was completely unprepared. For the stage, I was a Master of Fine Arts. For the camera, I was an illiterate. I was thrown by the demands of film style, and my performance was an embarrassment.

This book is the result of spending the next seventeen years trying to make up for that awful beginning. I offer it with the hope that no one will ever have to go through what I did, so many years ago.

—Richard Brestoff

Contents

Introduction

For the "Newcomer," the camera is usually intimidating—in my case the camera fixed its "eye" on me and within me all impulses, instincts, and thoughts raced to some secret, safe space—all the while I continued to talk and move about. I came to the sound stage totally uninformed, a stranger in a foreign land, unable to speak or understand the language. The customs eluded me, the people were unrecognizable.

And so I learned to dread, to fear, and finally to hate that "eye" that way through me to my secret hiding place, to my fears, to my inadequacies, and "so forth and son on and all the rest of it" to quote Chekhov. Eventually I learned, thanks to director Jules Dassin, who saw through my sham, recognized my dread and determined to teach me what Richard Brestoff is also determined to teach—"what they never told us" about acting for the camera. This book is more than terrific, it's needed.

—*Olympia Dukakis*

Illustrations

Chapter 3: Breaking Into Pieces

1. The Master
2. The 2-Shot
3. O.T.S. What the camera sees.
4. O.T.S. What the actor sees.
5. O.T.S. What a bystander sees.

Chapter 6: The Next Shot's in the Glass

6. Freeze frame
7. Marks
8. A call sheet
9. The 180° rule

A Better Way

You're sitting in a theater as a play is about to begin. Everyone is buzzing with excitement. Soon, the lights dim, talking stops, and the house is plunged into darkness. Your heartbeat quickens with expectation. But before the lights come up again, a voice speaks from the blackness.

"Ladies and gentlemen, we're going to try an experiment tonight. Something unusual and different. Instead of watching our performance from the restricted confines of your reserved seats, we are going to ask you to move about the theater anywhere you'd like to go. Feel free to wander around as the show is going on.

"We invite you to come up on the stage and stand next to, or behind the shoulders of, or even between the actors.

"You may lie on the stage if you like, or take advantage of the clear Plexiglas platforms we have built above the stage for overhead viewing.

"You may run from one spot to another, walk around slowly or pick a spot and stay there.

"Please change your viewing position as often and as little as you want. Tonight, we're taking off the shackles! You are liberated. Do with your freedom as you wish. Thank you very much, and enjoy the show." A murmur goes through the audience as the director leaves the stage. The shackles are off. Liberation. This is something different, indeed.

As the play begins, you want to explore your new found freedom. First, you walk to the back of the house to get an overall sense of the setting of the play. On your way, you accidentally bump into some other audience members who are quickly making their way to the front to watch from there. You only miss a little bit of the stage action and dialogue because of this. A bit of a disruption, but not too bad.

From your new position, the set looks really wonderful. It is an achievement in itself. Unfortunately, your view is partly obscured by the people on the stage and on the Plexiglas platform above the stage. Well, you didn't intend to stay back here anyway, so you shrug your shoulders and decide to join the anarchy up front.

You gamely fight your way forward, and happily find yourself right next to an actor. Being so close is great. Every expression is so clear and vivid. You wonder how the other actor is reacting to the angry tirade you are watching, but you cannot see the other actor very clearly. Working your way around other audience members, you finally arrive at an ideal spot. But just as you get there, the actor leaves the stage. You're not sure what to do next.

The actor who just exited is now backstage complaining to the director.

"I can't do any of my blocking because people are in the way, some of them actually talk to me saying that I'm screaming in their ears, while the ones further back say they can't hear me at all, I can't even see Roger, Bridgette is in tears, some idiot broke one of our prop dishes and cut himself, Mark says he won't go on, and I'm so distracted I don't even know what play I'm in!"

The director looks out to see what is happening. Instead of the chaos just described, however, he sees people quietly watching the play. Some are lying on the stage, others are back in their reserved seats. He tells the distraught actor that things have calmed down and to proceed as usual. The actor reluctantly goes back. Look at that, thinks the director, they're right back to sitting down again. I gave them their freedom, and they didn't want it. Maybe there's a better way, he wonders. He walks slowly out the back of the theater, and into the street. What's the matter, he asks himself as he walks. What went wrong, what happened to my experiment? I've got to clear my head, he thinks. He stops. Absent-mindedly, he hands some money to a ticket-taker. Is there a better way, he wonders as he takes his seat in the movie house. Yes, there must be a better way.

Chapter 1

Stealing The Soul

In our culture we take the presence of the camera so much for granted that we tend to forget just how magical an apparatus it is. So powerful is it, that some peoples throughout history have feared that it could literally steal their souls. Think of it. A person stands in front of a camera, a shutter opens, light enters, film is exposed and an image appears. What was there, is now here. Somehow, a part of a person has traveled across a distance and been captured. And more than captured, frozen. A photograph stops time. Forever and unchanged, there one is. Today, few of us believe that our souls have been stolen from us by the camera. But there are residual questions that show that this superstition still resonates strongly within us. Can the camera reveal secret parts of us even if we don't want it to? Is it just the film that is exposed, or is it our Selves as well? Does the camera possess the power to see into us like an x-ray of the soul, revealing both the beautiful and the grotesque? These questions are still with us, and are part of the reason that some people feel inhibited and protective in front of a lens.

The camera is an extension of our sight, and we think of the lens as an improvement on our eyes. It is capable of so much. It can show us the interior of a single cell, or the entirety of planet Earth . It can show an infinite variety of view points, can move or be still. When we watch a film, the camera stands for us. Through some wonderful alchemy of light, camera, recording medium and projection we can be transported to innumerable worlds, real or imagined. And yet, the camera is limited in some fundamental ways that we are not.

Our two eyes give us stereoscopic vision, which is what enables us to perceive depth. If you cover one eye, and look around with only the other, you'll find your ability to judge distances greatly impaired. Using two eyes means that we see in three dimensions; height, width and depth. The camera's one eye sees in only two dimensions; height and width. The truth is, the camera is a Cyclops living in a flat world. Even the film it records its images onto is flat. And to make matters even flatter, the movie and television screens its images are projected onto are essentially flat themselves. The illusion of depth is created only by the artistic use of light and shadow. The actor too must use a kind of psychological lighting and shading to give depth to his creations.

The camera does not discriminate. When we look at several objects, we can focus on one to the exclusion of the others. If these same objects are seen by the camera, special techniques must be used to highlight the one on which the filmmaker wants us to concentrate. In addition, our eyes are able to change focus from miles to inches instantly and without blur. To emulate this, the camera must rapidly rack focus on a zoom lens which involves the blurring of either the foreground or the background. In fact, much of the technical innovation involving the camera has been to make it function more like the human eye.

The only reason we see motion pictures as continuous at all is because of a peculiarity of our visual system. In 1824, Peter Mark Roget discovered that an image stays on the brain for one-fifth to one-twentieth of a second after it has been removed from the field of view. If you hold a piece of paper in front of your eyes and jerk it away quickly, you will see the after-image that Roget described and called *Persistence of Vision*. When films are projected at the rate of 24 frames per second, they are moving fast enough to blend after-image and new image into a continuous whole. Without *Persistence of Vision*, we would see a series of still pictures moving at a very fast pace without the illusion of continuous motion. But when the camera "sees" motion it is as a series of still images.

So, in some ways, the camera's viewing system is like ours, and some ways it isn't. Now, what about the question of our souls. Can it see into them? Can you fool the camera, lie to it? Or will it detect the truth no matter what you do? Let's do an experiment.

We have sixteen willing strangers in a room with a camera, a VCR, a playback monitor and a camera operator. We ask each one in turn to come forward, look into the lens and tell us three thing about themselves. They agree to do this. But when the first one comes forward, we whisper some special instructions to her that no one else can hear. We ask her to make one of the things she tells the camera a lie. Not an obvious lie, but a believable one. If her favorite color is blue, say it is red or green. If she was born in Detroit, Michigan say it was Chicago, Illinois. Something along those lines. She understands, and does as we asked.

When she finishes, another person comes up. But this time, we whisper something different. We tell this man to tell three things about himself but to make two of them lies. After he is done, another person comes forward. We whisper another variation to her; tell three truths. The next person is told to tell all lies.

After we shoot all sixteen of our volunteers, we gather around the monitor to watch the tape. But before we do, we give some instructions to the whole group. We tell them to imagine that they are a jury who must make a determination about which statements are true and which are lies based solely on the videotape testimony they are about to watch. They agree. We also tell them that different people were told to say different things.

We roll tape on the first participant:

"My name is Jenny, I was born in Portland, Oregon and I'm an architect."

We stop the tape. Well, we ask, what do you think? All truths, all lies, one truth and two lies, or two truths and one lie? Hands shoot up. All truth says one, and several agree. One truth and two lies says another, and several agree. Which were the lies, we ask. She wasn't born in Portland and she's not an architect, is the reply. No, says another. While I agree that there were two lies, I think they were her name and her occupation. Why do you think her name was a lie, we ask. Well, her eyes kind of looked off when she said it, like she wasn't really sure that was her name, is the answer. Another person disagrees altogether. He says there was only one lie and that it was about being an architect. He says she isn't. Several others agree. Finally, we ask the participant to sort it all out. She was really born in Santa Monica, California, and not in Portland. Not one person guessed correctly.

As we continue, we find this pattern repeating itself over and over again. While there are a few correct guesses, the volunteers find that they cannot reach any consensus and certainly not unanimity. This jury is pathetically unable to tell if a person is lying. In fact, this jury is even unable to tell if a person is telling the truth. The woman whose name is Jenny didn't convince some people that that is her real name.

The truth is, you *can* lie to the camera. It is not some kind of foolproof lie detector. If it were, politicians would avoid it like the plague, instead of seeking it out.

Yet, the whole truth is more complex than this experiment shows. We now know that the camera has no special ability or magic for screening lies, but we still don't know if it can see into the soul.

We ask our sixteen volunteers if they'd be willing to participate in another, more personal and risky experiment. Again, they agree.

This time, we tell them, they are at a funeral. They are to imagine that it is the memorial for a close loved one who has just died, and that they are here to deliver a eulogy for that person. This time, they are not to look into the camera lens, but talk about the loss of their loved one to the other participants, imagining them as friends and relatives of the deceased. If they have no one like this in their past, we ask them to eulogize a living loved one and imagine they have just died. Or, they may talk about the death of a relationship or the demise of a career. This experiment gives them the chance to say what may have remained unsaid for years. If strong emotions come up, we tell them, let them. If they do not, don't force them. Remember, we tell them, your task is to say what you've always wanted to say about this loved one, now lost to you.

Some eyebrows are raised, and some deep sighs go around the room, but luckily, we have found a group of very brave and committed people.

When the first person comes forward, she thanks everyone for attending this memorial to her father, and as she speaks, her painful memories of him evoke tears. She fights them back so that she can continue with her task. Suddenly, she bursts into laughter as she recalls a particularly funny incident. She catches her breath, and goes on. As she continues, her emotions swing back and forth like a pendulum. When she finishes, she is emotionally spent. Not every participant shows this much feeling, but when all sixteen are through, not a single person has seemed false or insincere. In the room, we are all moved by the eulogies and we wonder if the camera has caught and can project these same feelings. What will it be like as we watch for a second time on a flat screen?

As we watch the playback of the first participant's eulogy, we experience everything we did when watching her live. The camera has caught the truth of her feelings and can project them back to us. This happens for each of the sixteen. But, there is more to it than this.

When we ask people to comment on what they have seen, they speak not only of the genuineness of the obvious emotions, but of feelings that seem beneath the surface. Some say they sense great rage in one man, though it remained unexpressed. When we ask that man about such feelings, he says that yes, he did harbor tremendous anger toward his sister for leaving him when she died. Yet, sometimes, no hidden feelings were detected.

Let's step back and have a look at what happened in this experiment. First, everyone seemed genuine to everyone else during playback. We conclude from this that the camera *did* catch what was felt in the room. True feeling did survive the translation from three dimensions to two. Whatever a person allowed themselves to show was picked up on the tape. But there is more. Some people unconsciously revealed feelings that they hadn't intended to. Not that they were deliberately suppressing them, only that they weren't the primary emotions. Even the person who was unaware that any angry feelings had surfaced, could see them clearly on the tape. So, now, what can the camera see?

If by the soul we mean our inmost feelings, then, yes, the camera can see into the soul. But only if the soul will show itself. The man in our eulogy experiment wasn't aware that he had shown any anger, but he did. If the anger was buried deeply enough, it would not have shown, and the camera would not have picked it up.

Let's look at another example. We watch a newscaster doing the news. It never crosses our minds during the broadcast that this professional is in the least bit nervous. But a timely accident occurs at the studio and suddenly on screen we see that under his desk, this smooth anchorman's feet and legs are shaking furiously. Only this one portion of his body is telling the truth about his emotional state. Until we saw this nervous gesture, we had no idea that anything was going on beneath his calm exterior. The camera cannot reveal what it isn't shown. But it will pick up the most subtle and minute messages if given a chance. Can the camera see into your soul? It can. But you hold the key. Will the camera believe a lie? It will. If it is a believable lie. And a good thing too. If it didn't, actors would never be able to do their job; which is to create the reality of fiction.

There are other ways still by which the camera can give meaning to emotion.

On January 1st, 1923, a young scene designer, painter, and fledgling film director named Lev Kuleshov formed an experimental workshop for film actors and directors in a theater in Moscow. His most famous experiment involved the pre-revolutionary Russian film star, Ivan Mozhukhin. Kuleshov shot close-ups of the actor. In these close-ups, Mozhukhin displayed a neutral, expressionless face. Later, Kuleshov shot three other scenes without Mozhukhin in them. The first was a bowl of soup, the next was a woman lying in a coffin and the last was a shot of a little girl playing with her teddy bear. These scenes were then joined in different combinations with the close-up of Mozhukhin's face. V.I. Pudovkin in his book *Film Technique and Film Acting* remembers it this way: "In the first combination the close-up of Mozhukhin was immediately followed by a shot of a plate of soup standing on a table. It was obvious and certain that Mozhukhin was looking at this soup. In the second combination the face of Mozhukhin was joined to shots showing a coffin in which lay a dead woman. In the third the close-up was followed by a shot of a little girl playing with a funny toy bear. When we showed the three combinations to an audience which had not been let in on the secret the result was terrific. The public raved about the acting of the artist. They pointed out the heavy pensiveness of his mood over the forgotten soup, were touched and moved by the deep sorrow with which he looked at the dead woman, and admired the light, happy smile with which he surveyed the girl at play. But we knew that in all three cases the face was exactly the same."

What a startling experiment. The actor wasn't reacting to any of the scenes that were intercut with his close-up, yet the audience completely believed that he was and found his performance magnificent! Without him doing anything, great meaning was read onto his expressionless face. Today, this phenomenon is known as the *Kuleshov effect*. It states that emotional meaning in film is created by the juxtaposition of the shots. In the above example, the second shot (the soup, the dead woman, the little girl) gave meaning to the first

(Mozhukhin's close-up). Kuleshov concluded from experiments like these that "…in the cinema, the expression of an emotion by the actor does not depend on the cause of that emotion."

Early on in the making of a movie in which I was an actor, the director requested of an actress that she look off into the distance while he shot her. We were all seated in a classroom set, and the actress wanted to know what it was that she was supposed to be looking at. He didn't answer, but simply instructed her to do as she was told. She was confused. She wanted to know what it was that she was supposed to be reacting to and what it had to do with the scene we were shooting. He laughed and said it didn't matter what it had to do with the scene. All she had to do was look off, and he would take care of the rest. It's simple he said, just do it. His stubbornness confused her further. She said that all of a sudden she felt like a puppet and not at all like an actor. Actors need to know why they are doing what they are doing, she said. No, he replied, in film they don't need to know that at all. He asked her to trust him, and that when she saw the movie, she would understand and thank him. She said she felt manipulated and didn't like the feeling one bit. This disagreement went on for an hour, halting the production in its tracks. The director obviously knew of the Kuleshov effect, but none of the rest of us did. This resulted in an unfulfilling experience for everyone involved. Even if we had been aware of this technique, I don't think many of us would have wanted to use it much. Shooting this way can make the actor feel less than human and creatively useless. Such resistance may have even played a part in Kuleshov's questioning of the need for actors at all.

In the early 1920's, Kuleshov voiced his sentiments this way: "While the theater is unthinkable without actors, the cinema does not need actors…has no use for actors." I'm sure many directors and producers have felt the same way. Kuleshov went so far as to advocate the use of real people rather than actors in his films. Using real people who looked right for the part, meant that false theatrical acting would be eliminated from the cinema. This idea, embraced wholeheartedly by the great Russian film director Sergei Eisenstein, became known as *typage*. But when we watch the acting in many of Eisenstein's finest films it often appears stiff and unreal. The Russians soon abandoned this notion of typage and admitted the need for trained film actors. In America, typage became type-casting. Using actors, but ones that fit a preconceived idea of what the character should look like. And while it is true that everyone can be reduced to a type, no one is *just* a type. It is part of the actor's job to educate industry professionals to this fact.

While Kuleshov's experiment was remarkable, his conclusions were less so. Further experiments have shown that the Kuleshov effect doesn't always work as intended. If a man goes to a window and looks out with an inexpressive face at a shot of his wife and children lying dead on the ground below, the audience does not automatically read great grief into his expression. Rather, some will be repelled by the callousness of that very neutrality. What Kuleshov did discover was the power of altering circumstances in the editing room. In some ways, the whole idea is not too surprising. If we look at the Mona Lisa and are told that she is smiling because Da Vinci is painting her while he is naked, we will understand her smile in one way. If, however, we are told that she is suffering great physical pain, and that her smile is a brave attempt to cover it over, we will understand her expression quite another way. Changing the circumstances around a neutral or ambivalent expression does change the meaning of that expression.

Kuleshov's experiment shows that the camera can fool us, our truth and lie experiment shows that the camera can be fooled, and our eulogy experiment shows that the camera can transmit true depth of feeling. Can the camera steal your soul? No. But it can help to reveal it.

Chapter 2

Leaning On Walls

Some directors are afraid of actors. They are afraid that theater training has made them too stiff and "big" to be believable on screen.

The movie *Car Wash* was the first film I was in. Very early in the shooting, there was a scene in which I was supposed to be leaning against a wall. After looking through the lens, the director, Michael Shultz, asked me what I was doing. I explained to him that I was leaning against the wall. No you're not, he said, you're ACTING leaning against the wall. You don't have to do that here. In a theater, sure, if you really put your full weight against a flat it might fall over, and if you don't exaggerate a bit, the people in the back row might not be sure what you're doing, but, Richard, this is a REAL wall at a WORKING car wash. You can really lean against it. It won't fall down. Go ahead, try it, he said. At first, I was tentative. I wanted to make sure the camera could "tell" that I was leaning. So, I posed against the wall, not really sinking into it, not trusting it. No, Michael shouted. Lean against it as you would if we weren't here, as if you were alone and no camera was around. Slowly, I let the wall support me. You mean I can really do this? I asked. Yes, that's it, Richard, good, he said. Well, I thought, if I can really be here against this wall for real and not "act" leaning against a wall, then that changes everything. If I'm in a real place, then I don't have to project my voice. I don't have to "act" talking, I can just talk. I don't have to "show" the camera that I'm listening either, I just have to listen. All this happened in a split second, but it occasioned a revolution within me.

In *My Life In Art*, the great Russian director, actor and teacher, Constantine Stanislavsky, tells of an experiment he tried with some members of the Moscow Art Theater. While walking along the banks of the Dnieper River in Southern Russia, they entered the grounds of an old palace. One spot reminded them of the scenery from the second act of their production of Turgenov's *A Month In The Country*. They decided to try this act right there " . . . in the midst of nature." As Stanislavsky recalls: "My turn came, and now Knipper-Chekhova and I, as we were supposed to do in the play, walked along a long alley-path, repeating our text, and then sat down on a bench, according to our usual mise-en-scene, and – I stopped, because I could not continue my false and theatrical pose. All that I had done seemed untrue to nature, to reality . . . How far we are from simple human speech, how conventional we saw what we had become used to on the stage, considering our scenic truth to be real truth."

For Stanislavsky, there was no longer a set suggesting nature, this was nature. He was no longer an actor on a set, but a person in a garden. So, he couldn't merely "suggest" that he was a character, he had to be the character. His theatrical manner did not fit the reality of his whereabouts, and so seemed false. By "acting" that I was leaning against a wall, I too was violating the truth of my surroundings. Stanislavsky and I were both attempting to overcome obstacles that no longer existed. The need simply wasn't there to make sure the set didn't fall down, or to project to a distant audience. The reason actors appear too big and sometimes false on screen is that they are trying to overcome non-existent barriers. If we allow ourselves to accept the outer reality of where we are, then our inner reality will match it.

But does this mean that only a realistic and intimate style will work for the camera?

Actors are all too aware of the revolution in acting brought about by Montgomery Clift, Marlon Brando and James Dean in the 40's and 50's. Their personal and naturalistic style has dominated the screen ever since. Yet history shows us that there is no such thing as a single camera acting style. Actors have been successful on film using a variety of styles, from slapstick to deadpan, from intimate to broad. As long as they are believable, a large voice and a theatrical physicality are filmic. George C. Scott's performance in *Patton* is a case in point. Jose Ferrer in *Cyrano de Bergerac*, Bette Davis in *The Little Foxes*, Christopher Lloyd in *Back to the Future*, James Cagney in *The Public Enemy*, Laurence Olivier in *Richard the Third*, Albert Finney in *The Dresser*, Orson Wells in *The Third Man*, Peter O'Toole in *My Favorite Year*, these are all highly theatrical and successful film performances. If the directors of these films had been afraid of "bigness," these great performances would have never made it to the screen.

Sometimes, the same actor uses different styles in different films. Compare Al Pacino's intense performance in *The Godfather* with the theatricality of his performance in *Scent of a Woman*, or Robert Duvall's in *Tender Mercies* with *Apocalypse Now*, or Robert de Niro's internal portrayal of Travis Bickel in *Taxi Driver* with his theatrical posing in *King of Comedy*. If you were to ask these actors about these different styles, they would probably say that they weren't playing any style at all, but only the appropriate truth of that particular character.

A look at Sidney Lumet's film *Dog Day Afternoon* illustrates this point. In it, Al Pacino and John Cazale present contrasting styles based on the different characters they play. Sonny (Pacino), and Sal (Cazale), are both nervous wrecks as the result of a botched bank robbery attempt. But their responses to this calamity are completely different. Sonny is all agitated energy, externalizing his inner anxiety. Sal, on the other hand, withdraws into himself, trying to get hold of his rising panic. One could characterize Pacino's performance as externalized and Cazale's as internalized. But the truth is, both actors are working from a base of inner truth and reveal two opposite human reactions to fear and danger; fight (Sonny), or flight (Sal).

Both performances work as well within the confines of a single movie because they reinforce each other. Sal's paralyzing fear makes Sonny's manic action more necessary, while Sonny's furious handling of the situation allows Sal to retreat within himself.

Dog Day Afternoon not only shows how well different styles can work together, but gives us a wonderful example of actors thinking in terms of opposites. If both Pacino and Cazale had decided to portray their character's responses in the same way, there would have been no need for two characters at all. It is the contrast between them that makes interplay between the characters possible.

So, an intense, intimate style works on camera, and a big, theatrical style works on camera. The common denominator between them is believability. How is this achieved? Before dealing with that, let's look at the film shooting process itself.

Chapter 3

Bits and Pieces

Today, films are most often shot, edited and presented in what is known around the world as the *Classic Hollywood Style*. It emerged over time, and reached its current form in the late 1930's. It is a style modeled on the narrative techniques used in the great and popular novels of the nineteenth century.

These novels usually begin with expository material introducing the reader to the time, the location, and to the characters of the story. Next, the author explores the situation that the characters are in, and shows us the conflicts with which they must deal. If the reader cares enough about these characters, he will want to read on further to find out what happens to them. As the pace of events quickens, the interest of the reader increases. Soon, the reader begins to hang on every word, every gesture, every reaction, every twist and turn of the plot. As the conflict intensifies and the story reaches its climax, the reader's involvement is total. Then the conflict is resolved and tension is released as the writer places the story back into its context. The author has artfully drawn us into this world step by step. The progression of our interest has moved from mild curiosity to intense identification; from background to foreground.

Like authors, filmmakers are also tremendously interested in the techniques of arousing and sustaining audience attention. They know that a viewer must first be intrigued enough by something to want to come closer. So, the classic Hollywood film, like the novel, usually begins with explanatory material revealing the "what," "when," and "who" of the story. This is done in many different ways of course. Some films establish these things over the opening credits. Some take quite a long time with introductory scenes (*Howard's End*), some plunge the viewer straight into the middle of the action (*Raiders of the Lost Ark*), and then settle back for explanatory material. Whatever the case, films are generally structured around the novelistic techniques of exposition, complication, development, climax and denouement. The general movement is from the background context to the foreground main characters. Even scenes are shot this way.

The classic Hollywood shooting style begins with the shot furthest from the actors, known as the master, and ends with the shot closest to the actors, known as the close-up.

Between these distances are the two-shot (closer than the master) and the over-the-shoulder shot (closer than the two-shot). When a scene is shot on a set, the sequence of shooting is this: 1. *Master* 2. *Two-shot* 3. *Over-the-shoulder (O.T.S.)* 4. *Close-up.* This is done so regularly as to take on the aspects of a ritual. This may be so, because it mirrors the process by which a story-teller draws an audience into a story; from far back, to closer in. On sets every day, all over the world, film crews are unconsciously reminding themselves of what it is they do: tell a story.

It is crucial for film actors to understand that the moving of a camera from place to place is not simply the result of an arbitrary directorial decision. The actor needs to know what each shot is "telling," and how it helps to illuminate his character's story. Knowledge of the logical and psychological reasons for camera positions transforms the actor from a photographed object, to a creative collaborator.

The *master* gets its name from the fact that it records a scene from beginning to end and therefore serves as a reference shot. If all other coverage (any shot other than the master) was accidentally to be lost or destroyed, the entire scene could still be seen in the master.

The master.

For the actor, the master shot has some particularly important features. Since it is far enough away to hold all the actors and their surroundings in the frame, it is extremely useful for showing the relationships between the characters themselves, and between the characters and their environment. The actor doesn't need to "act" like she is in a restaurant, the audience can already see that. She doesn't need to "show" that she is cold, the audience can see the snowstorm for themselves.

Being a long and uninterrupted shot, the master also gives the actor the opportunity to find the timing with her fellow actor(s). Use the master to feel the contours and dynamics of a scene, its movement and rhythm. It may be the only time you can do this. You can't be sure that any other set-up will cover the scene from beginning to end.

Before the *camera blocking* (the movements of the camera) can be set, the crew and director must see the *actor's blocking* (the movements of the actors). This is one of the few moments when the actors and director can work on the scene together. If the actor has ideas about the scene, about where to be and when to move, now is the time to share them. The rehearsal for the master may well be the first time the actors have a chance to feel out the set, and work with the actual props. After the master is shot, the blocking will be very difficult to change. The other set-ups will be based on what the actors do in this shot.

How is the master used when the scene is edited together? That depends on the director and the content. If the scene edited is an intimate one, the master might only be useful at the beginning and at the ending. If, however, the scene involves a good deal of movement, be it broad physical comedy, or intense dramatic action, it might play entirely in the master.

So, the master is the reference shot into which the footage from all the other set-ups will eventually be inserted. For the actor, this means that any physical actions recorded by the master during the scene, must be matched precisely in all the other shots. If they are not, the different set-ups will not cut smoothly together. If you pick up a fork with your left hand when you say "What?", you must pick it up with the same hand and at the same speed and on the same line in all the other shots as well. This is called *matching actions* and it is a crucial part of the actor's job. When the editor and director cut from one angle to another, they will choose a moment in the *master* when the actor is beginning to reach for that fork, and match it with that same reach as it was recorded in the *two-shot*, for example, so that the reach for the fork is finishing in the new angle (the two-shot). This movement on the cut serves to disguise the fact that a cut was made, and makes the action appear continuous. The more exactly the actor matches his gross movements from angle to angle, the more precise and smooth the cut can be.

Now, let's look at the *two-shot*. Psychologically, the audience is moving in. It's as if one is eavesdropping on an interesting conversation in a restaurant, and decides to walk over to the other table and watch for a while. In real life, one would be quickly noticed and rebuffed. But in the *reel* world, the characters never become aware of the viewers' presence. This audience invisibility fulfills the viewers' wish to "be a fly on the wall" during the most interesting moments. The darkness of the movie theater is like the cloak of invisibility from fairy tales.

In the two-shot the viewer is more interested in what the characters are doing and saying. The focus is on the foreground because the audience is already aware of the scenic context. Consequently, more of the actors' bodies take up the frame.

The two-shot.

The two-shot serves as a transition distance between the further master and the closer over-the-shoulder. In some film and television today, the two shot is used as a master, or is eliminated altogether. The audience is sophisticated enough to accept the jump in distance from the master to the over without a feeling of discomfort.

For the actor, the two-shot presents another opportunity to feel out the interplay and timing of the scene. Being closer than the master, the actor can be more sure that facial expressions and body language will register.

The next set-up places the viewer closer, even intimately close. No longer content to watch and listen from a few feet away, the viewer now has the audacity to sit down behind one of the characters and peer over his shoulder! In the foreground of an *O.T.S.*, there is just a piece of one character. Usually a shoulder or a part of the head which takes up only a small portion of the frame. Just across from this is the full face of the other character.

O.T.S. What the camera sees.   Same O.T.S. What the actor sees.

Now we can see what we really want; how the character is feeling and reacting. In fact, we are almost in the scene itself. If the character reveals something of importance, we'll be here to see it. The actor can be sure that facial expressions will register at this close distance. It is also easier for the audience to understand what the actor is saying because the lips are so easy to see. After the eyes, the most watched part of a person's face is their mouth. Since the over-the-shoulder is shot from each character's point of view, it involves two set-ups; one from over each character's shoulder.

Same O.T.S. What an off-camera bystander sees.

In the *close-up* shot, the viewer is brought completely into the scene. And although the character is not looking directly at us, we have almost replaced the other character by moving inside his space. Only a loved one or a doctor gets this close to another human being. The character's face fills the screen and we are brought directly into the circle of his innermost thoughts and desires. In the close-up, the character may reveal an intimate secret, or try to conceal one. The character might make a confession, or remain silent. One way or the other we are there to witness it.

The close-up evokes a complex response in the audience. The viewer is in the paradoxical position of identifying with both the character speaking, and the one listening. For a moment, we are both characters. We begin to wonder, as we listen to the revelations of one, if the other is reacting to what they are seeing and hearing as we are. Our curiosity is at its height and we long to see how each character is feeling about the other. Thus, this shot, like the over-the-shoulder, is recorded from both points of view. As we watch the exchange of close-ups, we find our allegiances, expectations and identifications shifting. The close-up involves the most powerful interplay within the character himself, between different characters, and even between the characters and the audience. It is the closest the actors ever come to looking directly at the viewer. They don't, of course, because if they did, our cloak of invisibility would be lost.

So, we have four different basic shots; the master, the two-shot, the over-the-shoulder and the close-up. But we have six different set-ups; one master, one two-shot, two overs and two close-ups (one from each character's point of view).

In Kuleshov's workshop, they were forced to make films without film because the Russian civil war appropriated the materials from which film was made. Let's shoot a scene on paper as he did and see how all this might go together. The scene to be acted and shot is this:

1 INTERIOR APARTMENT – EVENING

(A woman is seen sitting alone at a table. A man enters.)

WOMAN

Hi, how are you?

MAN

Fine.

(He gets a drink from the refrigerator.)

                        WOMAN
What happened today?

                        MAN
Nothing much. (He sits.)

                        WOMAN
Oh.

                        MAN
You?

                        WOMAN
Nothing.

                        MAN
Want some?

                        WOMAN
No thanks.

                        MAN
Susan?

                        WOMAN
Yes?

                        MAN
Nothing.

We'll start, naturally, with the master. We set the camera far enough away so that it can catch the action of the whole scene from beginning to end. The actors play straight through from "action" to "cut." They have to do the scene three times before the director is satisfied.

Now we reposition the camera for a two-shot. Since the characters are together at the table for most of the scene, we set the camera to cover that area. The director wants the actress to begin the scene for this set-up with the line "what happened today," so that the man can "sit" into the shot saying "nothing much." Why does the actor need to sit into the shot? To disguise the cut, answers the director.

Another hallmark of the Classic Hollywood Style is *continuity editing*. This means that filmmakers want the audience to experience the illusion of continuous action undisturbed by jumpy cutting. The filmmaker does not want the audience to be aware of the fact that they are watching bits and pieces joined together. They fear that such an awareness would divert the viewers' attention from the story being told. So, ways have been developed to keep the viewer from noticing a cut. Early filmmakers discovered that if there is movement on a cut, the audience watches the motion and is distracted from the splice. Our director wants the actor sitting into the shot, so that he will have a smooth cut in the editing room.

The two-shot continues to the end of the scene. The actors and crew need four takes this time to get a print.

Now we position the camera over the man's shoulder so that we can see the woman's face. The director picks the scene up again from the same spot. We stay on her until the end of the scene. This time the director is satisfied with the first take. We reposition the camera over the woman's shoulder next, so that we can see the man's face in a matching shot. The director isn't happy until the fourth take.

Since we are already pointed toward the man, we move the

camera in for his close-up. We pick up the dialogue again at the same place. Three takes later, the scene is printed. Finally, we reposition the camera for the woman's close-up, picking up the dialogue at the same spot. Two takes later, the scene is finished.

When the scene is edited together, it looks like this:

MASTER:

> WOMAN
>
> Hi, how are you?

> MAN
>
> Fine.

> (He gets a drink from the refrigerator.)

TWO-SHOT:

> WOMAN
>
> What happened today?

O.T.S. – OVER WOMAN ON MAN

> MAN
>
> Nothing much.

O.T.S. – OVER MAN ON WOMAN:

> WOMAN
>
> Oh.

O.T.S. – OVER WOMAN ON MAN:

> MAN
>
> You?

TWO-SHOT:

> WOMAN
>
> Nothing.

                          MAN
      Want some?

O.T.S. – OVER MAN ON WOMAN:
                        WOMAN
      No thanks.

CLOSE-UP ON MAN:
                          MAN
      Susan?

CLOSE-UP ON WOMAN:
                        WOMAN
      Yes?

CLOSE-UP ON MAN:
                          MAN
      Nothing.

MASTER:
      No dialogue here. This shot emphasizes the
      missed communication between the characters.

This is not the only way to shoot or edit this scene. Many other choices exist. If we change the context of the scene, the content and meaning of it will also change. Suppose the man had just been fired from his job, or the woman had just been diagnosed with a terminal disease, or the man had just discovered that the woman has been having an affair? These circumstances would dramatically alter the acting of the scene and thus would affect the way it was shot. We also haven't explored combination shots and the moving camera.

The point to make for the moment, however, is that the actors have had to do the scene, or most of it, seventeen times. In some ways, of course, this might seem an advantage. The actor gets to do the scene over and over again until he gets it right. But there can be a false comfort in this. While matching actions and emotional intensities is important, they cannot be matched *exactly*. For this reason no two takes are precisely the same. One *never* gets to do the *first* take again. When it's over, that opportunity is gone. The second take is really the first try at *that* take, and not a repeat of the first one.

The difficulty for the actor lies in staying alive during all these multiple takes and avoiding the trap of becoming mechanical. How can one stay believable and spontaneous when this is the reality? Let's see.

Chapter 4

Taking It Personally

The first time we read through a script, we immediately picture ourselves in the part. We then usually spend the rest of our preparation time trying to recreate that image. But when we do this, we skip a crucial step necessary to the creation of what we want. This step is usually called PERSONALIZATION.

Personalization is the technique by which an actor explores his own unique responses to the material. It is an early part of our work in which we are not required to fulfill the demands of the text. In personalization, the words are only there for the actor's self-exploration. In this part of the process, the actor can be truly selfish.

First, cross out all stage directions, including emotional indications like "she cries," or "he looks wistfully out the window." If possible, sit across from your scene partner and begin the words of the scene. This occurs without movement (blocking), props, or costumes. The actor has no obligation at this stage to do anything that the scene requires. If what the actors say makes them laugh, then they laugh. No response is inappropriate. The only requirement is that the responses be genuine. If the actress' line indicates that she is talking to a man she finds unappealing, but the actress finds her scene partner attractive, she must play the reality in front of her. The line may then come out as ironic or as an obvious lie. In this way, the actress can free herself from any preconceived notions she may have about how the scene "should" be played. In the personalization process, actors constantly surprise themselves.

I was hired to play the part of a priest in an episode of *thirtysomething*. The character was trying to help Elliott (played by Timothy Busfield) deal with his wife's cancer. When I came to the set, I had a firm idea of how I wanted to play the scene. I went to Busfield's trailer to meet and rehearse with him. Soon after introducing ourselves, we started talking about religion. After a while he asked me if what I was saying was how I felt personally, or how I thought my character felt. I was at a loss for words. I wasn't sure. He said, "I see what we're doing. We're rehearsing." It was true. Without using the words of the scene, we had entered its territory. The dynamic was quite a bit different from how I had planned to play the scene, and yet what we were doing was so much more alive. When we finally got on the set, we simply carried on the interaction we had started in his trailer, only this time, using the dialogue of the scene. I threw out my preconceived ideas, and went with what was happening between us. I was no longer sure if I was talking to Elliott or Timothy and it didn't matter. The name meant nothing, only the person. The camera, the lights, the many distractions, meant nothing. Only the interaction between us held any meaning. If I had been unwilling to let Timothy affect me, I would have missed the truth of the scene between us. This is not to suggest that one throw out all one has prepared. This could be just as disastrous as missing the moment. What I am suggesting is that actors remain flexible so that they are not blinded to new possibilities.

Personalization, however, is only the first level of the actor's craft. Unfortunately, some actors never leave this level of work.

And while they can achieve a wonderful spontaneity and charm on screen with it, there is a danger. By playing only moment to moment feelings in each scene, these actors often miss the scene to scene consistency necessary to the development of their character. To do that, they must work at the next level.

Chapter 5

Riding A Horse

Acting is a verb. It is to do. Actors need to know what characters do, and what needs, wants and desires drive them. Careful analysis of a script allows us to make these discoveries.

There is a lot of confusing jargon surrounding the concepts we will talk about in this chapter. Some people use words like objectives and super-objectives, some use terms like intentions, actions and character spines. These words are all aimed at the same thing; an understanding of what a character is doing, and what a character wants in every line, scene and story. We will use the terms line objective, scene objective, plot objective and character objective to describe what a character wants, the word obstacle to describe what keeps the characters from getting what they want, the term strategy to describe how characters get what they want, and the words victories and defeats to describe if they succeed of fail. That's a lot of jargon. But, you wonder, must we? Is this analysis stuff really necessary?

Laurence Olivier once likened the process of acting to the racing of a horse. A horse, he said, is pure instinctive power; like one's personal and unique inner talent. But in a horse race, that pure power never wins by itself. The horse whose rider has fallen off always comes in last. That power, that instinct, needs guidance in order to focus on a goal. For the actor, that guidance is provided, he said, by analysis.

The great Polish theater director, Jerzy Grotowsky, put it another way. He likened the personal instinctive power of an actor to a river. But, he says, a river needs river banks to know where to flow. The guidance that these banks provide is like the textual analysis an actor uses to channel his talent. Without it, we often find ourselves directionless; desperately hoping that inspiration will rescue us.

Boundaries are often freeing. That is the paradox. If you are told to play a game, nothing will happen because you must pick a certain game in order to play. A game with certain rules. Within these rules, one is free to play. Without them, one doesn't know what to do. Too much freedom is paralyzing. Script analysis is the tool that we use to find the rules of a script, and to free ourselves from indecision.

The words on a page are like sunspots on the sun; surface manifestations of deep inner workings. They are like the tips of icebergs, like an architect's blueprints or like notes on sheet music. Geographers say that "the map is not the territory." They mean by this that the lines and dots and symbols on a map are not the same as the real dirt roads and living cities for which they stand. A script too is only an indication, a series of vital signs, but not life itself.

At the personalization level, we were not concerned with the demands of the text. At this level, however, we are.

To begin with, we want to know what the character wants with every line of dialogue. In other words, we want to discover the character's line objectives. The best way to state an objective is as a simple, action statement: To drive to the shore; get a drink of water; make him leave; tell her the good news; make dinner; make him cry. These are all action statements using verbs.

The first line of *Hamlet* is said by the character of Bernardo, a castle guard coming on duty. "Who's there?" he says. Already this is a bit odd, because the guard on duty, Francisco, should be challenging him. But knowing what has gone on before helps us to understand this. This is called a preceding incident. On two of the nights before the opening of the play, the ghost of the recently dead King Hamlet has appeared right where Bernardo stands guard. When he asks "who's there," Bernardo fears that what he sees in the darkness might again be the ghost. So, what is his line objective? Simple: to find out who is there. You ask a question to get an answer. And the answer to this question is very important to Bernardo. Does he find out who is there? The reply to him is, "Nay, answer me, stand and unfold yourself." No, he doesn't find out. His effort to fulfill his line objective is defeated. If the play ended here, it might be called Bernardo's Frustrating Night. But because Shakespeare overwrites, there's more. He must be somewhat relieved to have heard the voice of Francisco the guard he has come to replace, but Bernardo is still cautious enough not to reveal who he is. Instead, he gives a password: "Long live the King!" he replies. His line objective here is to show that he is a friend, not an enemy. Now Francisco has been defeated in finding out who the approaching person is. Bernardo did not "unfold himself," he just gave a password. If the play were to end here, it might be called I Won't Tell, You Won't Tell. But the play goes on. Francisco finally asks him straight out: "Bernardo?" Does he get an answer? Yes. Bernardo answers, "He." The beat is over and the title of this little playlet is, Thank God It's You. There is much to explore here.

Why wasn't the guard on duty, Francisco, doing his job? Why wasn't he aware of Bernardo's approach? Did Bernardo sneak up because he feared that he might run into the ghost? Was Francisco distracted by some activity or thought? What is Francisco doing before the opening of the play? An actor's first beat does not necessarily begin with the first words he speaks. A crucial part of our craft lies in creating life before the curtain goes up. What is the character doing? Waiting for the lights to come up? No. A bit later in the scene, Francisco says that it is "bitter cold." Perhaps he has built a fire and has been off gathering wood. Perhaps he has been preparing a warm drink at the fire and because of this, didn't hear Bernardo. Maybe he is simply lost in his own thoughts. Whatever, the actor must be thinking about these things before the first line of dialogue is even spoken.

After identifying the line objectives, the actor is ready to see where they point. This leads to the discovery of the scene objective. When Francisco tells Bernardo "For this relief, much thanks," we begin to get the idea. He doesn't want to be there. He wants to go home. Wanting to leave is a strong and playable objective. It involves a simple action: going. So why doesn't Francisco leave then? There is an obstacle in his way. What keeps him there? His duty. Until his watch is over, Francisco must guard the castle. He has a choice, though. He could just run off and face the consequences. But no, Francisco sees it through despite his desire to go. Whenever a character acts in a way that contradicts their objective, a clue to that character can be found. Despite his wish to leave, Francisco does his duty. This tells us something about Francisco's character. Indeed, a few lines later Marcellus calls him an " . . . honest soldier." Honest. That's what he is.

To some actors, the roles of Bernardo and Francisco are so small as to require no thought. And yet, if they were to apply this basic craft work to the parts, they would find great riches. This is what Stanislavsky meant when he said that there are no small parts, only small actors.

So, adding up line objectives leads to a scene objective. And adding up scene objectives leads to a plot objective. A look at all of Hamlet's scenes, leads one to conclude that his plot objective is to kill Claudius, his father's murderer. But he takes a great deal of time to accomplish this. His delay, in fact, has motivated centuries of speculation about his character. What does Hamlet really want? What is his character objective? If his character objective is the same as his plot objective, he would kill Claudius right away. Yet, one could argue, there are obstacles in his way. He must overcome them before he can take his revenge. This would be a legitimate way to see the part. Both the plot and the character objectives would be fulfilled at the conclusion of the fifth act.

But what if the character objective lays outside the boundaries of the play? Suppose Hamlet is secretly glad of his father's death. Perhaps his character objective is to dance on his father's grave. Perhaps as he jumps up and down on it, he shouts, "There, are you satisfied now? I'm a killer, a real man like you wanted me to be. Ophelia is dead, Polonius and Laertes and Rosencrantz and Guildenstern and Claudius and Gertrude are all dead. Are you satisfied? Is this what you wanted?" Perhaps he wants to be a man utterly different from his father. Perhaps his torment is due to the fact that he has been commanded to act against his nature. Perhaps his character objective is to escape Denmark. He does lament that "all Denmark's a prison." A character objective that lies outside the boundaries of the script can help us to create a living breathing human being that lives on after the theater goes dark.

One of the reasons that Marlon Brando's characterization of Don Corleone is so successful in *The Godfather* is that we can easily imagine him doing things that he doesn't actually do in the film. We can imagine him hanging a picture, building a bird house, setting the dinner table, all sorts of things that we don't really see him do. How is this accomplished? One way we have of achieving this is by placing an effective character objective outside the script. Sometimes the character himself is unconscious of this objective, and yet it informs everything he does. Perhaps Don Corleone wanted the same respect accorded to other great business men like Henry Ford or John D. Rockefeller. Maybe he wanted to prove to his father that he was a big shot. Maybe he just wanted a better life for his kids. Whatever the case, deep desires like these can help make a performance indelible.

But character objectives shouldn't be arbitrary. That can be dangerous. They need to be based on evidence from the material. Sometimes we get a sense of the character objective from our first reading of a script. Such an instinctive response is very valuable. It may hold a deep and important insight, but it needs to be checked against the text. Working on objectives is not as schematic as it appears on paper. Often we find ourselves working on two or three levels at one time; checking a line objective here with a scene objective there, or an overall strategy in this scene with an overall character objective. We must always be checking ourselves, testing our decisions against our instincts.

The simpler and more active an objective can be stated, the more playable it will be. In *Roots 2*, Marlon Brando plays George Lincoln Rockwell, the leader of the American Nazi Party, a racist and a hate monger. This part has "monster" written all over it. But the character doesn't think of himself as a monster. That's an outside judgment. So, how do you play it? Well, you act hatefully. But what is acting hatefully? Well, it's putting a scowl on your face because all the hatred inside has made you sour and bitter. But is any of this playable? No.

Brando has thought more deeply and more simply.

When Alex Haley (played by James Earl Jones, Jr.) comes to interview Rockwell, he is greeted in a startling manner. Brando/Rockwell takes a can of aerosol deodorant from beneath his desk, and slowly sprays the room with it. As he does this, he smiles and almost winks at his nearby lieutenant. With this simple act, Rockwell lets Haley know that he thinks black people have an offensive odor. The insult is brazen and unmistakable and it is meant to be a deep and painful one. But spraying the deodorant can is only one of the several strategies Brando/Rockwell uses to affront his guest. Many more are gleefully delivered throughout the course of the scene. The reason (or objective) becomes clear. Rockwell wants Haley to lunge across the table and attack him. Then he can claim that black people are savages who are unable to contain their sub-human impulses. At the end of the scene, Rockwell sings him one of the Party's theme songs. It goes: "The niggers are through in '72, parlez–vous?" Throughout the scene, Brando/Rockwell keeps looking over at his aide as though the two are sharing some great joke. The Nazi leader continues to taunt him, but Haley never rises to the bait. At the end of the scene Rockwell looks disappointed and no longer knows what to say or do; his strategies have failed. But Brando's have succeeded, for what emerges from his series of actions, reactions and strategies is truly the portrait of a monster.

In Martin Scorsese's *King of Comedy*, Robert De Niro plays Rupert Pupkin, another character in relentless pursuit of his objective. Rupert wants to perform his stand-up comedy act on the Jerry Langford show. That's what he wants, and he'll do anything to accomplish it. Rupert tries many ways to get on the show but fails. Finally, he kidnaps Langford and makes his appearance on the show the ransom required for Langford's release. De Niro's performance is a study in the single-minded pursuit of an objective. The way he waits in an outer office for his chance to see Langford is a lesson in itself. It is full of the little actions a person goes through when waiting. Most actors "wait" by sitting still and waiting. But De Niro knows that "waiting" is a general state composed of many smaller moments. He engages the receptionist in small talk, checks his watch, analyzes the ceiling, changes his seat, watches people come and go, shifts his body to get comfortable and engages in a myriad of activities that add up to what is generally thought to be the inactive state of "waiting."

Yet some critics and audiences find De Niro's performance in this film too cartoon-like for their liking. Why? When actors pursue objectives without showing the moments between them, without registering the defeats and victories between actions, a quality of "humanness" is lost. People usually show some feeling and vulnerability when they win or lose something of importance to them. Rupert does not. He mostly moves from action to action without showing victories and defeats. It was probably De Niro and Scorsese's intention to present the character this way. They are, after all, showing the behavior of an extreme social misfit, and it is a hallmark of people like this that they often lack the same feelings as you and I. De Niro and Scorsese probably felt that to humanize this character would be like "explaining" Rupert. This would run the risk of reducing him to a banal psychoanalytic type.

Rupert is a successful and disturbing characterization because De Niro and Scorsese keep us out of his inner life. This blankness arouses our curiosity and holds our fascination. It is a fine line to walk however, and while it works fairly well in *King of Comedy*, it fails in Scorsese's later remake of *Cape Fear*.

In *Cape Fear*, De Niro again plays a character obsessed with his objective: take revenge on the man who betrayed him. And again, the character hardly ever reveals his feelings about the victories and defeats that follow his actions. He simply goes from strategy to strategy until he gets what he wants. Because of this, his character becomes less a human being and more a force of nature. Instead of a character exacting his revenge, he becomes Revenge itself. No doubt this is what the actor and director intended, but playing a force, an abstraction, or a symbol is a difficult thing for an actor to do. Many critics and audience members find De Niro's characterization in this film unbelievable for this very reason. Compare De Niro's portrait of a "monster" in this film with Brando's in *Roots 2*. Brando's is the more chilling creation because he humanizes the monster, invites us to identify with him, and thus presents us with the uncomfortable truth that we are capable of the same ugliness.

So, acting is not just pursuing an objective, and it is not just playing the moment. Good acting results in the coming together of one's personal uniqueness with the text. The horse with the rider, the river in its banks. But doesn't all this preparation destroy spontaneity? Doesn't analysis inhibit intuition and imagination? When it intrudes on a performance and we can see the wheels turning, the answer is yes. As Spencer Tracy said "Acting is fine, just don't get caught at it." But when it is part of preparation, analysis actually frees the imagination. Knowing that good work has gone into the creation of a performance, means that an actor can trust that he is well prepared and open himself up to the reality and inspiration of the moment.

Now it's time to see how all this comes together. So let's take a look at the real Reel World.

Chapter 6

The Next Shot's In The Glass

The man at Newcomer's door hands him a manila envelope. "Your script," explains the messenger. "Oh right," Newcomer replies as he takes the envelope, "Thanks." Do I tip the person or not, wonders Newcomer. But when he looks up, the messenger is gone. Wow, thinks Newcomer. They messengered me a script! Amazing. Feeling almost as good as when his agent told him he got the part, Newcomer settles into a comfortable chair and opens the envelope. He stares at the title page of the script inside, *Baptism By Fire*. How appropriate for Newcomer's first camera job. In pencil at the top is his name. Wow, he thinks, I really did it.

Attached to the front cover is a small handwritten note. It tells Newcomer that his first day of shooting is four days away and that only one of his three scenes is scheduled to be shot that day: Scene 27. He rifles through the script to that scene. Nothing's been changed. It reads just like it did at the audition.

SCENE 27 – INTERIOR HALLWAY

DOUG

Hey, wait a sec!

> KATHY

Doug, it's over.

> DOUG

One more chance, that's all I want!

> KATHY

Doug, you just don't get it, do you? The answer
is no!

(Kathy exits. After a beat, Doug follows.)

O.K., thinks Newcomer, that's fine. This shoots Friday. But
when on Friday? Newcomer begins to panic. It doesn't say
when on Friday and it doesn't say where to be on Friday either.
Newcomer dashes to the phone and calls the production
company.

> RECEPTIONIST

Production.

> NEWCOMER

Yes, hello. This is Newcomer calling, and I'm
playing the part of Doug in *Baptism By Fire?*

> RECEPTIONIST

Yes?

> NEWCOMER

Well, I just got my script and it doesn't say
where or when to be on Friday.

> RECEPTIONIST

Hold, please.

NEWCOMER
O.K.

RECEPTIONIST
Thanks for holding. The information you need doesn't come from us. The call for your first day work comes from your agent.

NEWCOMER
Oh.

RECEPTIONIST
After that, your call will be given to you on a call sheet or by the 2nd A.D.

NEWCOMER
Oh. I didn't know that.

RECEPTIONIST
That's quite all right. Good-bye.

NEWCOMER
'Bye. (He hangs up.)

But what's a Second A.D.? Newcomer wonders. And what's a Call Sheet? Who can I ask? I can't let anyone know I'm this stupid! Newcomer decides to call his agent.

AGENCY
Whim and Fickle Talent Agency.

NEWCOMER
Hi, it's Newcomer. Do you have my call time and location for my first day of shooting on Friday?

> AGENCY
>
> Well, Mr. Newcomer, you're kind of jumping the gun.

> NEWCOMER
>
> I am?

> AGENCY
>
> Yes, it's only Tuesday. We won't get that information until late Thursday.

> NEWCOMER
>
> Oh, I see.

> AGENCY
>
> After that, your calls will come from the 2nd A.D.

Newcomer sees a chance.

> NEWCOMER
>
> Right. The 2nd A.D. That's the, uh . . .

> AGENCY
>
> The 2nd Assistant Director.

> NEWCOMER
>
> I know.

> AGENCY
>
> All right. Gotta go. Toodle.

> NEWCOMER
>
> O.K. 'Bye.

Ah, ha! The Second Assistant Director. Newcomer wonders how many there will be. Maybe he'll even find out about a Call Sheet before Friday. Maybe not. Newcomer tells himself not to worry about such things. Think about the script. That's what matters. Of course, he doesn't want to over think it. Or over worry. So for the next three days Newcomer reviews the line, scene and plot objectives for a while, daydreams the part for a while, tries not to think about it for a while, and sleeps for a while. Not that he sleeps too well. His dreams are full of anxiety. In them, he arrives on a distant set, and doesn't know where to go or who to talk to. When he finally does find someone, he can't be heard. In fact, no one seems to see him at all. He screams and yells, all to no avail.

Thursday night, his agent calls. He is to be on distant location at 6:30 a.m.

The next day, Newcomer arrives fifteen minutes early. He follows the map he has been sent to the crew parking area and gets out of his car. No one is around. He waits. Still no one. Panic rises. What am I supposed to do, he wonders. Something's gone wrong, he thinks. They've forgotten him. He's in the wrong place. He wants to cry. His nightmare is coming true! He thinks he's blown it, and begins to doubt his worth as an actor. He never belonged in the big leagues anyway, he thinks. A van drives up.

> VAN DRIVER
> You Mr. Newcomer?

> NEWCOMER
> Yeah, that's me.

> VAN DRIVER
> Get in, I'll drive you over to the set.

NEWCOMER
Oh, thanks. Thanks a lot.

The driver saw and heard him! The nightmare isn't coming true. Newcomer feels tremendous relief, even exhilaration. It's not yet 6:30 and already he's been through a week's worth of ups and downs.

Newcomer gets out of the van and sees bunches of people. Some are bustling about while others are standing around and talking. Some glance at him, but soon turn back to what they are doing. No one comes up to him, or even seems to know who he is. Well, here we go again, he thinks. He feels like an idiot just standing there, so he begins wandering around aimlessly. He stops, realizing that he doesn't have a clue as to where the actual shooting is going on. It's now 6:30. Resolutely, he walks up to the nearest person.

NEWCOMER
Excuse me, but I'm an actor and, uh, is there someone I should check in with?

NEAREST PERSON
Are you an Extra?

NEWCOMER
I don't think so.

NEAREST PERSON
Do you have lines?

NEWCOMER
Yes.

NEAREST PERSON
Then you're a Principal.

NEWCOMER
Oh.

NEAREST PERSON
You should report to a Second.

NEWCOMER
Right, of course, a Second Assistant Director.
Do you know where I'd find one?

NEAREST PERSON
Well, there's three of 'em on this set. They're
always wearin' walkie-talkies, you know.

NEWCOMER
Sure.

NEAREST PERSON
There's one. That's Stacey.

NEWCOMER
Oh great. Thanks.

As Newcomer heads for the Second, she spots him.

STACEY
Newcomer?

NEWCOMER
Yes.

> STACEY
> Right on time. Glad you found it. Let me take
> you over to your trailer.

> NEWCOMER
> Great.

A trailer! Wow, thinks Newcomer. They walk to a side street where a long row of trailers are stationed. Shiny metal steps lead up to each door. Stacey takes him to the one with his name on it.

> STACEY
> Your wardrobe is inside, and your contract, W4
> Form and I-9 Form are too. Wait a second.

She listens to her walkie talkie.

> STACEY
> (Screaming;) ROLLING!

Everyone outside quiets down.

> STACEY
> (In a lowered voice:) You get a breakfast. What
> would you like?

> NEWCOMER
> Oh, uh, an egg sandwich?

> STACEY
> Any bacon? Wait a second. CUT! Go ahead.

> NEWCOMER
> Oh, no thanks.

                    STACEY
Meaning no bacon?

                    NEWCOMER
Right.

                    STACEY
Toast and juice?

                    NEWCOMER
Sure.

                    STACEY
I'll bring it over in a bit then.

                    NEWCOMER
Great.

                    STACEY
ROLLING!

                    NEWCOMER
Thank you.

Newcomer heads up the metal steps. My own trailer, he proudly thinks to himself. But his enthusiasm drops as soon as he opens the door. Inside, it's the size of a small walk-in closet. There's hardly room to turn around. Across from a small sink with a mirror above it, is a narrow uncomfortable looking bench with a dark blue pad on it. Hanging above the bench is his wardrobe. Five steps in, an accordion door hides a tiny space with a toilet in it. Newcomer stares. So this is what they mean by a trailer. As he steps in, he sees papers on the small shelf by the sink. Contracts. As he goes over to see if they say the same things on them that his agent told him, he feels a draft. He looks for a heater. He finds one on the ceiling and turns it on. Nothing. He tries different settings, but it refuses to do a thing. He sits down. He got up early, drove a long way, felt completely lost in the parking area. He's felt elated, depressed, excited, insecure, sad, happy, frustrated, overjoyed and now cold. And it's not even 6:45 a.m. The day has hardly begun and he's exhausted.

STACEY

Got your breakfast.

NEWCOMER

Great, come on in.

STACEY

Here you go. Try to fill out that paperwork before the day's out. That's your contract, W4 form, and I-9.

NEWCOMER

The W4 is for taxes, I know, but what's an I-9?

STACEY

It's an immigration form to check on your citizenship. Did you bring a passport, or a driver's license, or social security card, or birth certificate?

NEWCOMER

Yeah, my agent said I would need some of those things.

STACEY

Good. A passport is stand alone document, but if you don't have one, then I need to see a

STACEY (CONT.)
driver's license and one other form of I.D.

NEWCOMER
I brought my license and birth certificate.

STACEY
Perfect. When you finish the other stuff, give them to me.

NEWCOMER
Great. Also, I noticed that I don't have a belt for my costume pants. Who do I talk to about that?

STACEY
I'll get wardrobe, they'll fix it. Here's a call sheet for today. We didn't get everything from yesterday so some of it slopped over into today. Instead of being the second shot up, now you're the fifth. Probably looking at three hours before you work. No need to get into wardrobe or make-up yet.

NEWCOMER
Maybe I should get some sleep.

STACEY
That's not usually a good idea.

NEWCOMER
Oh, why not?

STACEY
Well, you're not too alert when you wake up,

Unfurnished Studios **CALL SHEET** All Calls Subject to Change

1st Unit _8ᵀᴴ_ Day of Shooting

Series		No. _0271_	Director _T. ABATEMARCO_	
Picture " _BAPTISM BY FIRE_ "		Date _6/30 — FRIDAY_		
Exec. Producer _D. Mc CLEARY_		Shooting Call Time _7 AM_	Condition _RAIN OR SHINE_	
Producer _P. FRENCH_		☒ Report to Location	☐ Bus to location	

Pages	Set Description	Scene No.	Cast No.	D/N	Location
1 ³/₈	INT. APT. CORRIDOR	48	5, 8	D	77 HOPE ST.
⁴/₈	INT. APT. CORRIDOR	27	3, 4	D	
²/₈	EXT. APT. HOUSE	103	9	D	
1	EXT. PARKING LOT	4, 5, 8	5, 9, 10	D	
2 ⁶/₈		91	5, 6, 9, 10	D	
					↓

5 ⁶/₈	Total Pages	**NO FORCED CALLS WITHOUT PRIOR APPROVAL OF THE U.P.M.!**

CAST #	CAST	CHARACTER	SWF	Make-up	Set Call	REPORT TO:
1	N. MADEIRA	RUTH	H	—	—	LOCATION
2	J. ELLIS	MAC	H	—	—	
3	DEBBY	KATHY	W	6 AM	8 AM	
4	NEWCOMER	DOUG	W	6:30 AM	8 AM	
5	D. PIKUS	ANNIE	W	6 AM	7 AM	
6	P. PARKER	TOM	W/N	—	—	
7	R. MARION	LOU	H	—	—	
8	R. SILVEIRA	FRIEDA	W	6 AM	7 AM	
9	L. FRENCH	BOBBI	W	11 AM	12 N	
10	M. KOROLENKO	OTTO	W	11 AM	12 N	↓

Atmosphere and Stand-ins		Call Time	REPORT TO:
BUDDY, PAM		6:30 AM	LOCATION

ADVANCE: _MONDAY - 7-3_
NEWSPAPER INSERTS
EXT. WINDMILLS 98 - 101

Newcomer's call sheet.

52

STACEY (CONT.)
and after a long nap, your face gets puffy.

NEWCOMER
I see. Thanks for the tip.

STACEY
Kind of cold in here, isn't it?

NEWCOMER
The heater isn't working.

STACEY
O.K. I'll have transportation look at it.

NEWCOMER
They're in charge of the heater?

STACEY
They're in charge of all vehicles and everything inside them. I'll send one of the drivers over to take a look at it.

NEWCOMER
Before you go, can I ask you another question?

STACEY
Shoot.

NEWCOMER
What's craft services?

STACEY
Food. Snacks and drinks. On set you'll see a cart with donuts, cereal, fruit, juice, coffee, and

> STACEY (CONT.)

other stuff on it. That's craft services. Jimmy, our craft services guy, is great.

> NEWCOMER

So, that's where my breakfast came from?

> STACEY

Nope. Catering truck. Craft services is for snacking. The catering truck is for meals. Like when we break for lunch later, that will come from the catering truck. Just tell them you're a Principal, and you won't need to pay. Anyway, you've got about three hours. Don't leave the area without letting me know where you are. I'll get wardrobe and transportation. See you later.

> NEWCOMER

Great. Thank you again.

> STACEY

No problem.

Stacey leaves. Wow, thinks Newcomer, 2nd A.D.'s are great! I'll never leave home without one. Next time I arrive on a set, the first thing I'll look for will be a Second. There is a knock at his door.

> STACEY

It's me, Stacey.

> NEWCOMER

O.K. Come on in.

> STACEY
>
> I just realized I didn't give you the new pink pages. Or did casting send them over last night?

> NEWCOMER
>
> No they didn't. I don't have any pink pages. My script is white and blue.

> STACEY
>
> Well, let's just add some color to it. Here are the latest rewrites.

She hands Newcomer the pinks.

> NEWCOMER
>
> Thank you, I think.

A man comes in the trailer behind Stacey.

> VIC
>
> Hi, transportation.

> STACEY
>
> It's the ceiling heater, Vic.

> VIC
>
> I'll get right on it.

He tinkers with the heater.

> NEWCOMER
>
> So these pink pages are a new rewrite?

> STACEY
>
> Not a complete one. Just check your scenes to

> STACEY (CONT.)
> see if they've been changed.

> VIC
> That's got it I think. This switch was struck.

> STACEY
> Thanks, Vic.

> VIC
> Anything for you, Stacey.

> STACEY
> Yeah, right.

> NEWCOMER
> Thanks.

> VIC
> You bet. No problem.

Vic leaves.

> STACEY
> Wardrobe'll be over in a bit, so stay put. Don't go anywhere without letting me know. Bye for now.

She listens to her walkie talkie.

> STACEY
> ROLLING!

She leaves. Immediately, Newcomer rifles through the pink pages looking for scene 27. His heart skips a beat when he sees it. It's been rewritten.

SC. 27 INTERIOR HALLWAY

DOUG
Kathy, wait a minute.

KATHY
Forget it Doug, it's over.

DOUG
One more chance, that's all I'm asking.

KATHY
The answer is no.

Newcomer reads it through again. In some ways the scene is the same, and in others, it's different. Newcomer's character has changed. He seems to face the crisis of Kathy's leaving more calmly. The emotion may be the same, but the expression of it is different.

The writer has written the character with more control over himself. Newcomer realizes that Doug is now somewhat stronger than he was in the earlier version. There's no exclamation point after the first line and instead of "hey," he uses her name. The "please" is gone too which makes him seem less pleading. This rewrite presents a more in control Doug. So does this change his first objective? Not really. He still wants to stop Kathy from leaving. Only now he seems to be using a different strategy. Doug is showing a more reasonable side to her. He's not going to be hysterical, he's going to show her some self possession, some maturity. So how's he going to stop her from just continuing down the hall? Before, he was going to use his emotional distress to stop her, but this rewrite doesn't really allow for that. Maybe if I grab her, Newcomer thinks, and force her to stop that will work. Of course, that isn't really a mature thing to do and it might only make her madder. No, that's not a very good idea. Maybe I could get in front of her and block her way. Yeah, that could work. If she keeps walking, I could just backpedal, and keep talking. At least it's a plan.

There is a knock at his door.

> VOICE
>
> Wardrobe!

> NEWCOMER
>
> Oh, right. Come on in.

A man enters.

> VOICE
>
> Hi, I'm John from wardrobe, and this is your belt.

> NEWCOMER
>
> Great, thank you.

> JOHN
>
> No problem, that's what we're here for. Looks like you've got some time, so you can hold off getting dressed if you want to.

> NEWCOMER
>
> Oh, O.K. I thought I'd wander around the set a little and see what's going on. Do you know where they're shooting?

JOHN

Sure, they're over on the second floor of that apartment house.

NEWCOMER

Great, thanks.

JOHN

No problem. I'll be in the wardrobe trailer if you need anything else. Oh, don't leave anything valuable in here. Keep your wallet with you or give it to props and they'll lock it up for you.

NEWCOMER

O.K., thanks. I hate to keep asking you questions, but do you know where make-up is?

JOHN

Come here.

He opens the trailer door and points out.

JOHN

That's the make-up trailer and next to it there is the wardrobe trailer. Oh, and make sure Stacey knows where you'll be if you leave here, O.K.?

NEWCOMER

Will do. And thanks again for all the help.

JOHN

No problem.

He leaves. Newcomer sees the apartment building where the

shooting is taking place and heads over to it. One of the hallways there will be the one in which his scene will be shot. The thought makes his heart beat a little faster. He goes into the building.

Inside, there are cables everywhere. He has no idea where they come from or to where they go. People too seem haphazardly strewn about and many seem functionless. The whole scene has an air of chaos about it. Newcomer notices some people going up and down a nearby staircase so he decides to try it. At the top are more cables and more people. It is more crowded and disorganized than the lower floor so Newcomer feels that he must be getting nearer the nerve center. A little ways down the hall is a food cart with a large coffee urn and some snacks on it. Ah, craft services! Newcomer heads over to it. Standing next to the cart is an elderly man with a light blue fishing cap on his head. Sharp blue eyes peer out from the brim. Newcomer reaches for a doughnut.

> MAN
> Better steer clear of those. Bad for you.

> NEWCOMER
> Sure look good though.

> MAN
> Have fruit. Got to be smart on a set. A lot of things working against you. Junk food doesn't have to be one of them. You an actor?

> NEWCOMER
> Yeah, I play Doug.

> MAN
> The kid having the fight in the hall with his girlfriend?

NEWCOMER
Right.

MAN
What's your name, kid?

NEWCOMER
Newcomer.

MAN
Mine's Peter. Nice to meet you

NEWCOMER
Nice to meet you too. You an actor?

PETER
For thirty-five years.

NEWCOMER
Wow, that's a long time.

PETER
Yep. Here, let's sit down.

NEWCOMER
Where?

PETER
See these chairs that say "cast" on them? They're
for us. We're cast.

They sit in low backed directors' chairs. Newcomer with an
apple, Peter with a pear.

PETER
You ever worked in front of a camera before?

NEWCOMER
Well, no. Not really. This is my first.

PETER
Well now, this calls for a celebration!

He goes to the snack cart.

PETER
Have a doughnut!

NEWCOMER
But you said . . .

PETER
One won't kill you.

He hands a jelly doughnut to Newcomer.

NEWCOMER
Thanks.

PETER
Listen, if this is your first camera type job, you're going to need help. I'd be happy to show you the ropes if you want.

NEWCOMER
That'd be great. I haven't told anybody about it being my first. I'm kind of nervous. Do you know what all of these people do around here?

PETER

Well, see that woman looking through the lens of the camera?

NEWCOMER

Yes.

PETER

That's the *camera operator*. She's the only one actually watching the scene through the lens. If you move around, she follows you. If the movement is side to side, that's called a *pan*. If the move is up and down that's called a *tilt*. It's a good idea to make friends with the operator. Since she's the only one actually seeing you through the lens, she can tell you if you've moved out of frame or not.

NEWCOMER

How do I make her my friend?

PETER

Good question. When she's not too busy lining up a shot, go up to her quietly and introduce yourself. Ask her if it wouldn't be too much trouble if she could let you know if you're leaning out of a shot or if you're blocking yourself with an arm or a prop or something. Tell her you want to make her job easier and that if there's anything you can do to assist her, just ask. The operator can be your best ally on a set. At a good moment, ask how much of you is in the frame. Just your head, or your head and neck, or your head and shoulders, or your head and chest or what. See, you might know it's your close-up, but a close-up means different things to different directors. You need to know what parts of you are being seen, and how much room you have move around in.

NEWCOMER

I see. So then, if she does all that, what does the Director of Photography do? Or is that same person?

PETER

Long time ago, they were the same person. But not today. No, the Director of Photography is standing by the actors wearing a light meter around his neck. The DP, as we call him, is in charge of the overall look of the film. He works with the director before shooting begins to find out how the director wants the film to look. He then chooses the film stock and the lenses, even the lab that will process the film. He hires the rest of the camera crew including the operator. He also helps the director decide how to shoot a particular scene and where to place the camera. But most important, he is in charge of the lighting. DP's paint and sculpt with light.

NEWCOMER

Is he the one holding the light meter to the actress's forehead?

PETER

That's him. He wants to expose the film and the subject to just the right amount of light to achieve the effect he and the director want.

> NEWCOMER

Could I ask him about my frame line and things like that?

> PETER

No. You don't want to bother the DP. Ask the operator about those type of things, or the director. Now, you see the man watching the DP?

> NEWCOMER

Sure do.

> PETER

He's the head of the lighting crew. He's known as the *gaffer*. The DP tells him what he wants, and he tells his crew where to put the lights and where to focus them and what kind of filters, if any, to use and things like that. Getting the lights right is what usually takes so much time on a set. His chief assistant is called the *best boy*.

> NEWCOMER

What if his assistant is a woman?

> PETER

(Getting up) You want some coffee?

> NEWCOMER

Actually, I would. With some milk?

> PETER

Coming up.

He hands Newcomer a cup of coffee.

PETER

By the way, you know never to spike the lens don't you?

NEWCOMER

I don't know what you're talking about.

PETER

That means never look directly into the lens during a scene.

NEWCOMER

Destroys the contract we have with the audience that they are invisible, breaks the "fourth wall."

PETER

So you do know something. Very good.

NEWCOMER

Read it in a book called *The Camera Smart Actor*.

PETER

Never heard of it.

VOICE

SO THERE YOU ARE!

Newcomer and Peter swivel around.

NEWCOMER

Stacey!

STACEY

Didn't I tell you to tell me where you are at all times?

NEWCOMER

Yes, you did. I'm sorry.

STACEY

We'd like you to get into your wardrobe now and then head over to make-up.

NEWCOMER

Now?

STACEY

Now.

NEWCOMER

I thought I had three hours.

STACEY

They moved your scene ahead.

PETER

Excuse me, but he's just not ready.

STACEY

Why, what's the problem?

NEWCOMER

Well, I . . .

PETER

He's just not ready that's all. Can't they shoot something else for a few hours?

> NEWCOMER
Hey, no. I can do it.

> STACEY
Are you feeling ill?

> NEWCOMER
No.

> STACEY
Well then, let's go.

Stacey and Newcomer start to walk off.

> PETER
WAIT!

He snaps his fingers. Everyone freezes in place except Newcomer and Peter.

> NEWCOMER
Hey, what's going on? Everybody's frozen!

> PETER
Well, there are still some things I have to explain to you.

> NEWCOMER
Yeah, like how this happened! Am I hypnotized or something?

> PETER
Or something.

NEWCOMER
Oh, come on. This is impossible!

PETER
Is it?

NEWCOMER
YES! It's some kind of a trick.

PETER
That's right, it's a trick. Why don't you come over to the camera with me while you figure it out.

Newcomer goes to the camera with Peter.

NEWCOMER
This is strange.

PETER
And as a stranger, give it welcome.

NEWCOMER
Sure. Right. Weird.

PETER
No more weird than movie making itself.

NEWCOMER
Oh, yes it is. It's weirder, you can bet on that.

PETER
Instead of worrying, you should take advantage of this time. Now look at this fella with his hand on the lens. Want to guess what he does?

NEWCOMER
Are they going to *un*freeze at some point?

PETER
Yes! Now will you stop worrying and try to focus on what I'm saying! What do you think this man does?

NEWCOMER
Mister, I don't have a clue.

PETER
He's the *focus puller*. When you're rehearsing for the camera, he measures the precise distance between the focal plane of the lens and your face. That way he can have you perfectly in focus. If you move to a different position, say you lean forward for part of the scene, he measures that distance and subtly readjusts the lens for that new distance.

NEWCOMER
The operator can't do that?

PETER
No. She's too busy following the action and keeping everything well framed. So now when someone sticks a tape measure in your face, you'll know what it's for. Now, see the camera is on a platform with wheels?

NEWCOMER
Yes.

PETER

Well, that's called a *camera dolly*. People aren't the only things that move during a scene. Cameras do too. Cameras have blocking just like actors do. This fella back here moves the camera to its marks. He's called the *dolly grip*. Grips are people who put their hands on things and move them around. If you move a chair or something during a scene, don't *you* put it back in its original position for another take. A *grip* will put it back on its mark. That's his or her job. Grips are also part of the lighting crew. They move the light poles around. The head grip is called the *key grip*.

NEWCOMER

I see. So let me get this straight. The focus puller is moving the lens, the operator is panning and tilting and the dolly grip is moving the whole camera into different positions.

PETER

Right.

NEWCOMER

It must be difficult to get all that together if the actors are moving around a lot themselves.

PETER

It is. that's why good camera actors learn to move a little more slowly than they do in real life. Even getting up from a chair can be hard for the camera to follow. So you do it more slowly than you usually would.

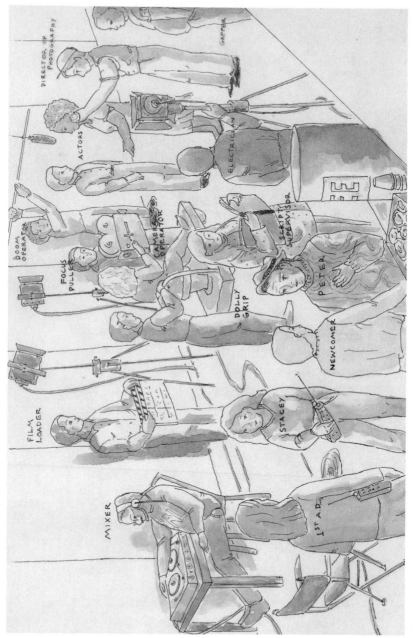

What a by-stander sees.

NEWCOMER

Uh huh. Are these people breathing?

PETER

Yes, they're breathing.

NEWCOMER

That's good.

PETER

Standing here is yet another member of the film crew. The *film loader*. A standard can of film holds about eleven minutes on it. So after that is used up, the camera has to be reloaded. That's the film loader's job.

NEWCOMER

Pretty specialized.

PETER

True. But unless there's another camera assistant, the loader has some other jobs as well. When you rehearse, he puts the marks down on the floor for the actors, and when it's time to shoot, he works the clapsticks.

NEWCOMER

Yeah, now what's the point of those? Clapsticks?

PETER

Well, you see, your performance is recorded in two different places. The camera gets your *body* on *film* but a tape recorder gets your *voice* on *tape*. Now these need to be synchronized. So, the editor lines up the *picture* of the clapstick

PETER (CONT.)

hitting the board with the *sound* of it striking from the sound tape. That way he knows that the sound and the picture are in sync.

NEWCOMER

Cool.

PETER

Even cooler are the new digital clapsticks.

NEWCOMER

What are those?

PETER

Clapsticks that show a number readout that helps the editor line up the sound and picture even more precisely.

NEWCOMER

Amazing.

PETER

Now, do you have any questions before we move on the sound crew?

NEWCOMER

Well, you mentioned about *marks*. I've heard a lot about hitting them, but I don't know how to do it or why it's so important.

PETER

Good. I'm glad you mentioned that. By the way, they only put marks down for rehearsals. During the actual shooting, they take them up.

                    NEWCOMER
Cruel, cruel.

                    PETER
True. Come over here.

They walk to the hallway and stand near the camera.

                    PETER
Now suppose you come out of this apartment
door here, after she's run out.

                    NEWCOMER
O.K.

                    PETER
Now suppose the director wants you to stop
right here.

He stops midway down the hall.

                    NEWCOMER
Yeah?

                    PETER
A mark will be set down for you to rehearse
with. They usually use white chalk or gaffer's
tape in two strips. One strip goes across and
one strip goes down to form a "T" shape. Your
feet straddle the line going down and your toes
go just behind the top cross bar, like this. Try it.

                    NEWCOMER
O.K.

He does.

PETER

Good. Now, you come out of the apartment door trying to save your relationship with your girl friend. You shouldn't be thinking about your mark, but how are you going to find it? Staying in frame depends on it, staying in focus depends on it, staying in your light depends on it. How are you going to find it?

NEWCOMER

Well, if I walk from the door over to the mark a bunch of times, maybe that will do it.

PETER

Try it.

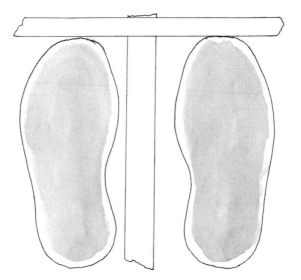

Toe Marks.

Newcomer goes to the door, turns around, and walks slowly and deliberately to the mark. after several tries he gets pretty close without looking.

> NEWCOMER
>
> With practice, this is no big deal.

> PETER
>
> Well, what you did is what most new actors do, and it won't work.

> NEWCOMER
>
> Why not?

> PETER
>
> You just very normally walked it. I bet you even counted the number of steps.

> NEWCOMER
>
> I did.

> PETER
>
> Right. Only you didn't walk it at *performance energy*. *How* are you going to be coming out of that door? Fast, slow? If you're really moving, your stride will be completely different.

> NEWCOMER
>
> Well, I'd probably be in a hurry to stop her.

> PETER
>
> Right. So now try it the way you'd really do it.

> NEWCOMER
>
> O.K.

Newcomer goes back to the door and this time hurries to the mark.

PETER

A lot fewer steps, right?

NEWCOMER

Like half as many! If I'd taken as many steps as I did the first time, I'd be out of the building.

PETER

Right. So always rehearse getting to a mark at performance level.

NEWCOMER

Yes, I see that.

PETER

Now, what you did is called *front stepping*. Some actors try to hit marks by doing just the opposite, *back stepping*.

NEWCOMER

What's that?

PETER

Well, you start on the mark and then walk backwards to your starting position. By the way, your starting position for a scene is called *number one*. If you hear the 1st AD say "back to *number one*," you go back to where you first were at the beginning of the scene.

NEWCOMER

O.K., I'll remember that.

PETER
Good. Now try backstepping the mark.

NEWCOMER
Right.

Newcomer begins on the mark and then hurries backward to the door.

PETER
Did you count the steps?

NEWCOMER
Sure did.

PETER
Now, start from the door and go to the mark in the same number of steps at performance energy.

NEWCOMER
O.K.

He does.

NEWCOMER
Geez, I overstepped it a mile!

PETER
Right. You see, your stride going backwards is shorter than it is going forwards.

NEWCOMER
So, backstepping is not too useful.

PETER

I would agree with that.

NEWCOMER

Then, front stepping a bunch of times is the best way to hit a mark?

PETER

Well, it helps. There's such a thing as muscle memory. Meaning that if you practice enough, your body learns where to stop. Only front stepping alone isn't enough.

NEWCOMER

That's too bad.

PETER

Go stand on your mark.

NEWCOMER

O.K.

PETER

Now, looking ahead and about at eye level, line up a near and a far object.

NEWCOMER

I'm not sure what you mean.

PETER

Like cross hairs in a rifle sight. From the position you're in, spot where something close by lines up with something on the wall back there.

NEWCOMER
Well, the corner of this light pole lines up with the bottom of the "E" on the exit sign on the far wall.

PETER
Good. When those are lined up, you're on your mark.

NEWCOMER
Really?

PETER
Well, with a little practice I mean. With the help of a little muscle memory.

NEWCOMER
O.K., let me try.

PETER
Be my guest.

Newcomer goes back to the door and heads to the mark at performance level.

NEWCOMER
Look at this! I'm right on it!

PETER
Yep. Now go back to the door.

NEWCOMER
O.K.

As Newcomer goes to the door, Peter removes the mark from the floor.

> PETER

Try it now.

> NEWCOMER

Yike.

> PETER

Go ahead, I know exactly where it was.

> NEWCOMER

O.K.

Newcomer goes, at performance energy, to where his body directs him and where the light pole and exit sign line up.

> NEWCOMER

This seems like it.

> PETER

Look down. I left a tiny piece of tape there.

> NEWCOMER

I'm right on it! I hit my mark!

> PETER

Call the Academy.

> NEWCOMER

Hey, this is great. Thanks a lot.

> PETER

Sure. So did you figure out how I froze everybody?

The Next Shot's In The Glass

NEWCOMER

No, I'm just going with it at this point.

PETER

Good man! Stay open. Remember, anything can happen in the movies.

NEWCOMER

Give me a break.

PETER

So, how are going to talk?

NEWCOMER

In the scene? Just conversational.

PETER

Got to be a little careful about that. If you don't give the sound people enough level, you might have to loop your dialogue later.

NEWCOMER

Loop? What's loop?

PETER

Redoing your dialogue months later on a sound stage. I don't have time to go into it now. Look it up in your book, it's probably in there.

NEWCOMER

I thought in the movies you could talk real low like Marlon Brando. You mean I have to project my voice even for a microphone?

PETER

No, not like on the stage. But you've got to give the mic something to record! Talk in your normal voice, that should be enough. But don't talk so low that they can barely pick you up. Because later on, when they boost the volume so audiences can hear you, the signal will be so weak that it will mostly be noise.

NEWCOMER

But in an intimate scene, can't I talk real low?

PETER

Yes you can, but the sound people will fight you on it. They'll ask for more level. And if it doesn't affect your performance, give it to them. But if it does, don't. Now I'm not talking here about *theatrical projection* and neither are they. Dialogue should sound real, likes it's been wiretapped. Come over here.

They walk over to a man wearing headphones who's sitting at a small cart on wheels with a tape recorder on it.

PETER

The man sitting here is the mixer, or sound recordist. He's the chief of the sound crew. His assistant is the boom operator. He's holding the boom over the head of that actress over there.

NEWCOMER

I see. They put mics on you sometimes too don't they?

PETER

Right. Radio mics. The boom operator hides the mic near a shirt button or somewhere, and then runs a wire inside your clothes to a battery-pack which they usually tuck into your back pocket.

NEWCOMER

That must feel a little strange.

PETER

It does. But then the boom operator doesn't have to follow you around everywhere, and there's no chance that you'll get out of the mic's range. The other common way to mic a scene is to carefully hide them around the set.

NEWCOMER

So, if I move, boom operator has to move with me.

PETER

Correct.

NEWCOMER

O.K. Let me see if I understand this so far. When I'm acting a scene, the camera operator is following me, the focus puller is keeping me in focus, the dolly grip is moving the camera dolly, and the boom operator is following me with the mic?

PETER

If the scene involves movement that requires all those things to happen, then yes.

NEWCOMER
Makes it kind of hard to improvise something
you haven't rehearsed, doesn't it?

PETER
Yes it does. Of course, the paradox is that you
learn all this and then forget about it while
you're acting.

NEWCOMER
Forget about it?

PETER
Sure. You should be thinking about the *scene*
you're about to do, not about all the technical
stuff going on around you.

NEWCOMER
Then what is the point in learning all this?

PETER
An actor who knows what's required by the
director and the crew is more secure, can
protect and improve his performance, and saves
everybody time. You know, film making is this
battle between time and excellence. If you are
an actor who saves a production some time,
then the possibility for quality increases.

NEWCOMER
Why don't they just take more time, and do
things right?

PETER
Money. Shooting costs money. Every project

has a budget. Look, in Network television a half hour show is usually given no more than five days of shooting. But an hour long show is *not* given twice as long, as you might expect. No. An hour show must be completed in *seven* days. That's an average of eight pages a day that they have to shoot. That means that the actors have time only to go with first choices. They don't have *time* to explore second and third approaches to a scene or a character. For the director it means that there's only time for three takes before he has to move on.

NEWCOMER
I see. Is it different in movies?

PETER
Yes. That's why everyone wants to do films. An average shoot day on a movie is around *two* pages. There's time to do a little exploring, time to do the number of takes you need to get the performance you really want. But even so, movies have budgets and schedules too. So, from the moment production begins, the pressure is on. A shooting day is one of the most expensive days on Earth. The quicker you get it done, the less it costs.

NEWCOMER
So if you have to stop and explain everything to an actor, you lose time and money.

PETER
Yes. But that doesn't mean you shouldn't question things you don't understand, or that

violate your sense of the truth of the scene or your character. Remember, it's a balancing act. Giving in totally to the time constraints means that quality hasn't got a chance.

NEWCOMER
So, you have to pick your spots. Choose your battles.

PETER
I think that would be wise.

NEWCOMER
Hey, I think the sound man's hand just moved.

PETER
Then I don't have much time. I can't keep this up forever. See this woman standing behind me?

NEWCOMER
Yeah.

PETER
She's the *script supervisor.*

NEWCOMER
Is she important?

PETER
You bet. Outside of the director, she's the most important person on the set. In her script, she makes special marks that show what type of set-up was shot (you know, a master, a two-shot, an over, or a close-up), how much dialogue the set-

PETER (CONT.)

up covered, how many seconds the shot took, how many takes there were, what went wrong on each take, which one was printed, any changes the actor's made in the dialogue, which hand the actor was holding a drink in, on what line the actor put the drink down, what coverage remains to be shot and many other things as well.

NEWCOMER

Wow. Is this also what they call the *continuity person?*

PETER

You got it.

NEWCOMER

She seems like a person I wouldn't bother. She's way too busy.

PETER

Busy she is. And to show you how important she is to a production, it is *her* script that goes to the editor at the end of the day. He or she uses *it* as the primary guide to editing the film.

NEWCOMER

Amazing.

PETER

But you're wrong about bothering her.

NEWCOMER

You're kidding.

PETER

No. You see, there's another aspect to her job. If you forget a line, or need help with lines, she's there to help you.

NEWCOMER

How can she possibly have time for that?

PETER

Well, a smart actor won't overdo this, but it is part of her job and she'll be glad to do it. If you're not sure of a line and your script isn't handy, ask her. If you need to know exactly what you said in a certain shot so you can repeat it in another, she'll know. If she has time, she'll even run lines with you.

NEWCOMER

So if I see she's not too busy, I can work with her.

PETER

Right. Not only that, but sometimes *she'll* work with *you.*

NEWCOMER

Meaning?

PETER

Meaning that if you have a scene where you're on the phone and the other actor isn't around to do the other end of the conversation, the script supervisor will read the lines. Or if the other actor isn't around for your close-up, the script supervisor will read the off-screen lines for you to act and react to.

NEWCOMER

O.K., a phone call I can understand. But why wouldn't your fellow actor be there for your close-up?

PETER

Some actors, not many, are so selfish that if they're not in the shot, they disappear.

NEWCOMER

That stinks.

PETER

I'm glad you think so.

NEWCOMER

So, have I met just about everybody I need to at this point?

PETER

Nope. There's the prop person, make-up and hair people, the 1st Assistant Director, and I guess that would cover you for now.

NEWCOMER

O.K. I know what make-up and hair do. I met the wardrobe person and a Second A.D., so maybe you could fill me in on props and the 1st A.D.?

PETER

Sure. If you wear a watch in a scene where do think it comes from, wardrobe or props?

NEWCOMER
Well, if I'm wearing it, maybe it's the responsibility of the wardrobe department?

PETER
Nope. The watch is a prop.

NEWCOMER
So, it comes from the prop department?

PETER
Right. Guns, badges, eye-glasses, pens, pencils, food, flashlights, all that kind of stuff comes from props. The prop people are also responsible for many special effects.

NEWCOMER
I didn't know that.

PETER
If there's an explosion that needs to be shot, the prop department sets it up. If you are supposed to be shot with bullets in a scene, the prop people will put little exploding devices called *squibs* on you. If smoke is required in a scene, they will provide it.

NEWCOMER
Wait a minute, I'm stuck back at the squibs. They put *exploding devices on you?*

PETER
To make it look like the bullet hit you, sure. It's a little scary at first, but they know what they're doing.

NEWCOMER

But haven't some actors been hurt and even
killed by screw-ups with those things?

PETER

Yes, that's quite true. You do have to be careful.
If you are supposed to do something or
something is supposed to be done to you, make
sure the prop person demonstrates what it is
first. Don't do anything that you don't
understand, or anything that hasn't been tested
first. When you feel comfortable that your
safety is assured, then go ahead.

NEWCOMER

So, I don't have to do anything dangerous?

PETER

No. There are stunt people and stunt doubles to
do the physically dangerous things. If they
really want you to do something dicey and you
feel it's O.K. and want to, be sure they
compensate you with what's called *hazard pay*.

NEWCOMER

That's extra money?

PETER

That's right. An extra risk means extra money.

NEWCOMER

Frankly, I think I'd be a little intimidated to ask
for extra pay.

PETER
What you do, is call your agent from the set.
They'll deal with it.

NEWCOMER
I see.

PETER
But 99% of the time you won't be asked to do
anything dangerous.

NEWCOMER
Good.

PETER
Now, see this woman standing by Stacey?

NEWCOMER
Yes.

PETER
Well, let me introduce you to the 1st A.D.

They walk over to the woman.

PETER
1st A.D., I'd like you to meet Newcomer.

Newcomer pretends to shake her hand.

NEWCOMER
How do you do, it's a pleasure. So what the
heck do you do?

PETER

She runs the set. She is the boss of everyone on the set except for the actors and the director. If she tells the crew to stop working, they stop. If she calls "quiet on the set," everyone gets quiet.

NEWCOMER

Oh, so that's who says that.

PETER

Right. The 1st is the director's right hand person. He tells the 1st what he wants and when he's ready to shoot, and the 1st takes over. After checking with the D.P. and the director, she calls for a rehearsal with the actors. When the rehearsal is finished, she calls for the *second team*.

NEWCOMER

What's that?

PETER

The second team consist of the stand-ins for the actors. There is no reason for the principal actors to remain in their positions while the lights are adjusted and focused and the camera moves are practiced. So, special people are hired to replace the actors while all this goes on. When they're ready to shoot, the 1st will call for the *first team*. That's you.

NEWCOMER

So then, the second team leaves, and we take over.

PETER

Right. There still might be some last minute
adjustments of the camera and lights, but
basically, it's time to shoot. At that point, the
1st A.D. will call for quiet on the set, then say
"roll camera," she'll then wait for the camera
operator to tell her that the camera *is* rolling
then she'll call "sound?", and wait for the mixer
to say "speed," which means that the recording
heads have gotten up to speed, then she'll call
for the scene to be slated, and then someone
will call "action!" Who would that be?

NEWCOMER

The director?

PETER

Absolutely right. Now, that's not all the 1st
A.D. is responsible for. She also helps plan the
next day's work schedule so a call sheet can be
ready at the end of the shoot day.

NEWCOMER

This is probably a stupid question, but does an
assistant director ever get to *direct*?

PETER

That's a good question. The 1st A.D. is
responsible for directing the extras. On a union
shoot, the director is not even allowed to direct
the extras, technically. That is the job of the 1st.
She tells them where to move and what to do.
Now, of course, the director tells the 1st what
he wants, but it is the 1st who talks directly to
the extras.

NEWCOMER
Now that's division of labor.

STACEY
NEWCOMER?

NEWCOMER
Oh, no! They're waking up!

PETER
Told you I couldn't keep it up forever.

People are starting to move around.

NEWCOMER
What am I going to do?

PETER
I'll be a voice in your head.

NEWCOMER
What does that mean?

STACEY
Newcomer, LET'S GO!

PETER
No time to explain. Good luck.

He walks over the craft services cart.

STACEY
NEWCOMER!

NEWCOMER
COMING!

Stacey hurries Newcomer down the stairs and out of the building.

> STACEY
>
> Make-up is waiting for you in that trailer.

> NEWCOMER
>
> Thanks. By the way, how are you feeling?

> STACEY
>
> A little hassled, but fine. Why?

> NEWCOMER
>
> Just wondered. So, do you know that guy I was talking to?

> STACEY
>
> What guy?

> NEWCOMER
>
> The guy I was standing with and talking to for half an hour?

> STACEY
>
> Didn't see him.

> NEWCOMER
>
> You didn't see him?

> STACEY
>
> No.

There is a pause.

> NEWCOMER
>
> Fine. Whatever.

The Next Shot's In The Glass

STACEY

You all right?

NEWCOMER

Not really, no.

STACEY

Well, get your make-up on and then hop into costume and maybe you'll feel better. And if you need, there's a nurse on set.

NEWCOMER

Sure, thanks.

Stacey and Newcomer head up the steps and enter the trailer. Disco music is blaring.

STACEY

Joel, this is Newcomer, and he's playing Doug.

JOEL

O.K. Newcomer, if you'll have a seat right here, we can get you started.

STACEY

Let me know when they're done.

JOEL

Yes, ma'am.

Stacey leaves. Newcomer has noticed a woman in another chair who is also being made up.

JOEL

So, what they want for you is a little color and a

JOEL (CONT.)
tan. Won't take but a moment.

NEWCOMER
O.K., great.

WOMAN
Excuse me, did I hear that you're playing Doug?

NEWCOMER
Yes, I am. Are you playing Kathy?

WOMAN
Yes, I am. How do you do? My name's Debby. Kind of strange to meet just a few minutes before a scene isn't it?

NEWCOMER
Sure is. Well, how do you do, nice to meet you, I'm Newcomer. Let's have a fight in a few minutes.

DEBBY
Right, you're on!

PETER
Look up please. Got to line those eyes.

NEWCOMER
O.K.

PETER (Voice Over)
Now's a good time to rehearse.

Newcomer's head jerks around.

JOEL

Oh, sorry. Did I get your eye?

NEWCOMER

What? Oh, no. I just thought I heard a voice.
Did you hear a man's voice?

JOEL

No, not really. Maybe it was the radio. I'll turn
it down.

He turns the music down.

JOEL

Now, eyes up please.

NEWCOMER

Right.

Newcomer looks up and then hears the voice in his head again.

PETER (V.O.)

No one can hear me but you. don't panic. I told
you I'd be a voice in your head, and here I am.
Now you just met the actress playing Kathy,
why not run the lines with her? Feel out the
relationship between you.

Newcomer sits quietly for a moment.

NEWCOMER

So, Debby, you want to run these lines?

DEBBY

Sure, we probably should do that.

As they rehearse the lines sitting in their make-up chairs, Newcomer realizes that Debby is playing Kathy with a great deal of anger. He finds himself responding in kind. This isn't how he had planned to play the scene. The new rewrite seemed to demand a cooler and less agitated Doug. But the intensity of Debby's anger is triggering his own. After a few times through, Debby suggests that they stop for now, and go over it again later. Newcomer agrees. As Newcomer leaves the make-up truck and heads to his trailer, a familiar voice enters his head.

> PETER (V.O.)
> She's coming on pretty strong isn't she? She's a good actress, but don't mirror her feelings in the scene. That's a classic mistake.

Newcomer goes into his trailer. Peter is there. Newcomer doesn't seem to notice, and simply goes right on.

> NEWCOMER
> But I should let myself be affected by her shouldn't I? I mean no matter what I planned I should let myself be affected by my scene partner, right? That's what I was taught.

> PETER
> Up to a point. Of course you must let the other person in the scene affect you, but not *dictate* your reactions. Effective scenes are often built on the *contrast* between the characters. Have you ever seen *Dog Day Afternoon*?

> NEWCOMER
> Yes, yes.

PETER

Well, then, since the rewrite suggests that Doug is more in control than before, you have a great reason for *underplaying* the scene. She'll be hot, you be cool. Don't be drawn into her mood.

NEWCOMER

O.K., I see what you mean.

Newcomer finishes putting on his costume.

STACEY: (V.O.)

(From outside Newcomer's door.) Newcomer, they're ready for a rehearsal!

NEWCOMER

O.K.! I'm coming.

Newcomer's heart is suddenly beating like a jackhammer.

NEWCOMER

This is it.

PETER

It's exciting! Take a few deep breaths.

Newcomer exits his trailer and walks with Stacey. Peter is nowhere to be seen.

STACEY

(Into her walkie talkie) He's about two minutes away.

NEWCOMER

How's everything been going?

STACEY

We're a couple days behind, and tempers are a little short, but basically pretty well.

They enter the apartment building and head up the stairs. A voice is heard in Newcomer's head.

PETER (V.O.)

Do you remember the director's name?

NEWCOMER

What's the director's first name again?

STACEY

Tony. His last name is on your call sheet.

NEWCOMER

Right.

She ushers him onto the set.

STACEY

Here he is, Jenny. Jenny is our fearless 1st.

NEWCOMER

Hi.

1ST A.D.

Good to meet you. Sorry about the change, but we had to move up your scene. The crane we needed for the exterior shot didn't show.

NEWCOMER

That's O.K.

> 1ST A.D.
> Would you step in please?

Jenny gestures toward one of the apartment doors. Newcomer heads over to it. A cluster of people hover around the door, talking and waiting. Newcomer hasn't seen the director since the audition two and a half weeks ago, and is embarrassed to discover that he can't recognize him. He stands near the door, unsure what to do. A man walks up to him.

> MAN
> How are you?

> NEWCOMER
> Oh, fine, fine.

> MAN
> Good. We should be getting started as soon as Debby gets out of hair.

The man opens the door and goes through, talking to Newcomer.

> MAN
> You'll start from in here and then follow her out into the hallway.

He comes back out the door and walks briskly down the hall.

> MAN
> Stop her about here after you say "wait a minute." Ah! Here she is!

> DEBBY
> Hi, Tony.

MAN

Good morning.

O.K., I thought so, thinks Newcomer, this guy is the director. Sure is in a hurry.

DIRECTOR

As I was telling Newcomer, I want you to start with a clean entrance from behind the door, and then he'll stop you about here. That'll be the first shot. Let's try it, and see how it works.

1st A.D.

QUIET, PLEASE! REHEARSING!

Newcomer and Debby go behind the door. This represents the room in which the scene *before* took place.

DEBBY

Maybe we should get into it by doing the lines from Scene 26.

NEWCOMER

Good idea.

DEBBY

O.K.

SCENE 26 – INTERIOR-APARTMENT LIVING ROOM

DEBBY as KATHY

It's over! I'm not staying a second longer! Good-bye.

NEWCOMER as DOUG
Look, I told you I was sorry.

DEBBY as KATHY
Too late. I'm gone.

Scene 26 is over.

DEBBY
And then I storm out the door.

NEWCOMER
And into the hallway scene.

DEBBY
(Laughing) Right.

DIRECTOR
(From the hallway) Let's see the action please!

Debby pulls the door open and storms out. A second later Newcomer comes out. But by then, Debby is halfway down the corridor and well past the place where the director had wanted them to stop.

DIRECTOR
Hold it! Hold it! Newcomer, you've got to come out much faster. Let's try again. And Debby, where's the suitcase?

DEBBY
I'm supposed to have a suitcase?

DIRECTOR

Well, since we're shooting out of order, we have to think backwards. In scene 26, when we shoot it next week, you'll be packing your clothes while you tell Doug you're leaving. So you would be coming out of the door in *this* scene with that suitcase in your hand.

DEBBY

That's a good idea. So when we shoot the *end* of scene *26*, I'll have to remember to be holding the suitcase in the same hand as I have it at the *beginning* of this scene *27*.

DIRECTOR

Right. PROPS!

PROP MASTER

Yes, sir?

DIRECTOR

Where is the suitcase for this scene?

PROP MASTER

In the room, sir.

DIRECTOR

O.K. Let's go again. Newcomer faster, Debby with suitcase.

1ST A.D.

Back to number one, for rehearsal. Hold the work!

Newcomer and Debby go back into the room just off the hallway.

> DEBBY
> (Spotting the suitcase) Oh, here it is.

She picks up the suitcase in her left hand.

> DEBBY
> Boy, I didn't even think of this. Shooting out of
> order is weird.

> NEWCOMER
> Yeah, you really have to think it out.

> DIRECTOR
> ACTION!

This time with suitcase, Debby storms out of the room and into the hallway. But this time Newcomer catches up to her at the right spot. They stand

> DIRECTOR
> To the dialogue please.

SCENE 27 – INTERIOR-HALLWAY

> NEWCOMER/DOUG
> Kathy, wait a minute.

> DEBBY/KATHY
> Forget it Doug, it's over.

The director directs.

> DIRECTOR
> And start to go, Debby.

She does.

> DIRECTOR
> And Newcomer you stop her as she turns.

Newcomer puts his hand on her shoulder as says his line.

> NEWCOMER
> One more chance. That's all I'm asking.

The director directs again.

> DIRECTOR
> Now, Debby, look over at his hand on your shoulder, and then look at him.

She does.

> DIRECTOR
> Newcomer, after she looks at you, take your hand away. Then, Debby, you say your line.

> DEBBY/KATHY
> The answer is no.

> DIRECTOR
> Then, Debby, you take off down the hallway, and Newcomer, after a beat, you follow her.

They go.

> DIRECTOR
> O.K., that's the scene. Let's show it to the camera.

Tony goes over to his director's chair, as the Director of Photography comes over and talks with him. There is a voice in Newcomer's head.

> PETER (V.O.)
> This is one of your few chances to have any input. If you have some ideas, voice them now.

Newcomer goes over to the director and D.P.

> NEWCOMER
> Um, excuse me, I don't mean to interrupt . . .

> DIRECTOR
> Yes?

> NEWCOMER
> Well, when we were rehearsing just now, it felt like it might be stronger if she took my hand off of her herself, instead of my removing it.

> DIRECTOR
> Maybe. Let's see it. Debby!

Debby comes over and Tony explains Newcomer's idea to her.

> DEBBY
> You know, I actually felt like doing that, but I stopped myself. Let's try it.

They do the scene this way and everyone likes it better.

> DIRECTOR
> Good. Now let's try to line up the shot.

> 1ST A.D.
Back to Number One!

Newcomer and Debby go back to the room off the hallway.

> DIRECTOR
ACTION!

This time as they come out, a team of people follows them down the hallway. Besides the director and the D.P., Newcomer recognizes the camera operator, the gaffer, the script supervisor and the 1st A.D. They stop where they did before.

> DIRECTOR
Good. Mark them.

> DEBBY
You know, Tony, I just don't think I would stop because he says to wait. I mean, I'm leaving. I'm out of here. I don't know. Maybe if he got in front of me, that might work.

> DIRECTOR
O.K., let's try that. Newcomer, cut her off right around this same place here.

> 1ST A.D.
Back to Number One!

This time down the hallway, Newcomer gets in front of her.

> DIRECTOR
Yeah, makes more sense, good. But as soon as she stops, turn sideways to her. That'll be a better shot for us.

Newcomer does.

> DIRECTOR
> Good. Mark 'em.

A man Newcomer recognizes as the second assistant camera man, or film loader, rips off strips of gaffer's tape, and makes "T" marks where they are standing.

> 2ND ASST. CAMERA MAN
> Now, where were you when you stopped, before
> you turned sideways onto these marks?

Newcomer and Debby show him. He again puts down "T" marks.

> 2ND ASST. CAMERA MAN
> O.K. these are your first set of marks, and these
> are your second.

> NEWCOMER & DEBBY
> Thank you.

> 2ND ASST. CAMERA MAN
> You bet.

He goes back to the camera.

> 1ST A.D.
> Second team! You two can relax.

As Newcomer and Debby step off their marks, two stand-ins take their places. Debby heads off to the craft services cart, with Newcomer following.

PETER (V.O.)
Excuse me, but now would be a good time to practice hitting your marks. Don't get in anyone's way doing it, but do it.

Newcomer continues to the craft services cart, and gets a cup of coffee.

PETER (V.O.)
Don't load up on that stuff.

NEWCOMER
All right, all right.

DEBBY
What?

NEWCOMER
Oh, nothing.

DEBBY
You want to sit down and go over the scene?

NEWCOMER
Yeah, in a second. First I'm going to walk these marks. I'll be back in just a few minutes.

DEBBY
That's a good idea. I'd do it too, except I take my mark from you. I'll be over in the "cast" chairs.

NEWCOMER
O.K.

The Next Shot's In The Glass

Newcomer heads back to his first position.

> PETER (V.O.)
> Very impressive. She thinks you're a veteran.
> Now do this at performance energy, but don't
> knock over the stand-ins or get in the way.

Newcomer speeds down the hallway and stops short of the
stand-ins. He notes how far he is from the walls, and which
door he is nearest. He then goes back to his first position and
does it again.

> PETER (V.O.)
> Good. You don't need to line up a near and far
> object yet because things are going to move
> around as they light. Go rehearse.

Newcomer heads over to where Debby is sitting.

> DEBBY
> Is it going to be hard to find?

> NEWCOMER
> The mark? No, I don't think so.

> DEBBY
> Well, this is going to be fun.

> NEWCOMER
> Well, I hope so.

> DEBBY
> You know, at first, I thought we should
> rehearse, but maybe we should just leave it
> alone and keep it fresh.

> NEWCOMER
>
> Well, it's not a long dialogue scene, and I think we both know it, so maybe you're right.

> PETER (V.O.)
>
> She is.

> DEBBY
>
> Well then, I think I'll just hang out in my trailer.

She gets up.

> NEWCOMER
>
> O.K., I'll see you soon.

> DEBBY
>
> That you will.

She leaves. Peter sits next to Newcomer, holding a half eaten apple.

> PETER
>
> Hello.

Newcomer jumps.

> NEWCOMER
>
> Geez! Look, who are you exactly? And where did you disappear to? And how did you get into my head? Are you real or am I nuts?

> PETER
>
> You're not nuts. Calm down. I'm here to help. I've been helpful, haven't I?

NEWCOMER

Yeah, and a little pushy.

PETER

I know. Sorry.

NEWCOMER

Look, can you give me some kind of explanation?

PETER

I'm a Wizard. Sent by the Screen Actor's Guild to help new actors on their first day of work.

NEWCOMER

Bull.

PETER

No good? O.K. I'm a small part of the Magic that *is* the Movies!

NEWCOMER

Quit it man! I'm getting a little unnerved. Who are you?

PETER

Sorry, can't say. You want me to leave?

NEWCOMER

Well, no. Not really.

PETER

O.K. then. Hang in there with me for a little while longer.

NEWCOMER

O.K.

PETER

Good. Now, you're in this strange limbo land of waiting while they light the scene.

NEWCOMER

Yeah. What am I supposed to do?

PETER

Stay level. If that means going to your trailer and playing the guitar, or staying on set and chit-chatting with people, fine. Just don't *waste* your energy. Waiting can be exhausting. And after a while, your performance drains away through your chair and spills out onto the floor. Shooting is exciting. Stay with that energy. Don't give it away, and don't bury it. Just *be* with it.

NEWCOMER

Sounds kind of New Agey.

PETER

It isn't.

NEWCOMER

How long does lighting take?

PETER

Depends. Anywhere from twenty minutes to a couple of hours. This'll probably take about forty minutes or so. Hallways aren't the easiest. Why don't you take a few quiet moments and look at your script.

NEWCOMER

I know the lines.

PETER

Not for the lines. Look at it and dream a little.
Watch it in your head.

NEWCOMER

I never did that before.

PETER

Yes you have. You just weren't aware of it. Go
ahead. Look at it and then close your eyes.

NEWCOMER

All right.

Newcomer looks at the scene and then stares off, as if in a
trance. The noises and distractions of the set fade away. He is
still for some time.

NEWCOMER

I watched it. I saw the whole scene. And the
scene before.

PETER

Yes.

NEWCOMER

It gave me some ideas, too.

PETER

Yes. Feel calmer? More centered?

NEWCOMER

I do.

1ST A.D.

1st team!

PETER

Let's see how long it lasts. Get going, 1st team is *you.*

NEWCOMER

Oh, yeah!

Newcomer hops out of his chair.

1ST A.D.

Quiet on the set! Back to number one please.

Newcomer and Debby go to their positions. Newcomer's heart is pounding again.

DIRECTOR

ACTION!

Debby comes out with Newcomer following. He stops her and they play the scene.

DIRECTOR

O.K. Can you hold where you are please? Is that a more natural place for you?

NEWCOMER

Actually it is.

DIRECTOR
O.K., re-mark them.

As the 2nd assistant comes over to re-mark their positions, Newcomer looks down to see how close to his mark he is. About four inches behind it. Newcomer is angry with himself. He hears a voice in his head.

PETER (V.O.)
Don't worry. These adjustments happen all the time. It's normal.

DIRECTOR
Stay on your marks please, so we can line up the shot.

NEWCOMER
Didn't they already do this with the stand-ins?

DEBBY
Well, you know they always have to do this fine tuning stuff.

NEWCOMER
Right. Always.

A man Newcomer remembers as the focus puller, or 1st assistant camera man, pulls a tape measure from the camera to his face. The D.P. comes over and hold a light meter to his forehead.

D.P.
He's too hot! Pop a single scrim in there, please. That's better.

The make-up man comes over.

> JOEL
> Time to touch you up.

He goes to work, while Newcomer continues to stand on his mark.

> PETER
> Might be a good time to introduce yourself to the camera operator.

Newcomer glances over, and notices that the operator is sitting quietly at the camera. Newcomer catches her eye.

> NEWCOMER
> Hi. I'm Newcomer. I'm playing Doug, which you probably already know.

> OPERATOR
> I do. Nice to meet you. I'm Joan.

> NEWCOMER
> Nice to meet you.

> DIRECTOR
> All right, let's rehearse one!

> 1ST A.D.
> Back to number one! Rehearsal!

Newcomer leaves his mark and goes up to the operator.

> NEWCOMER
> Joan, if I lean out of frame or go too fast, let me

NEWCOMER (CONT.)
know will you? (Joan nods her head.) Thanks.

Newcomer heads back to his first position. Debby is already
there. They both stand quietly, concentrating.

1ST A.D.
QUIET ON THE SET! REHEARSAL!

In a whisper, Debby begins the dialogue from the scene before.

DIRECTOR
ACTION!

Debby swings the door open and strides down the hallway.
When Newcomer comes out of the door, he says the beginning
of his line.

NEWCOMER
(At door) Kathy!

He runs down the hallway, finishing his line.

NEWCOMER
Wait a minute.

They get no further.

OPERATOR
Hold it, we got a boom shadow.

DIRECTOR
Stay where you are please.

> BOOM OPERATOR
How's this?

> CAMERA OPERATOR
Still see it.

The boom operator lifts the boom pole up.

> BOOM OPERATOR
Now?

> CAMERA OPERATOR
No good.

The boom operator twists the pole to one side.

> BOOM OPERATOR
Now?

> CAMERA OPERATOR
You're out!

> BOOM OPERATOR
Good, O.K.

> DIRECTOR
Look, let's try one for real, maybe we'll get lucky.

> 1ST A.D.
1st positions please, we're going to shoot this one!

As people go their places, the boom operator leans over to Newcomer.

BOOM OPERATOR
Could you delay your line at the top of the scene? I can't really pick it up back there at the door.

NEWCOMER
You mean when I say "Kathy"?

BOOM OPERATOR
Yeah. If you could maybe say that when you're further down the hall, then I could get a good level on it.

Newcomer thinks for a second.

NEWCOMER
Sure, I could do that.

BOOM OPERATOR
Thanks, that'd be a big help.

Newcomer goes back to his starting position. A hair-dresser is fussing over Debby, as Joel gets hold of Newcomer.

JOEL
Just a final check.

He lightly powders Newcomer's face.

1ST A.D.
QUIET ON THE SET!

Newcomer's heart is racing again.

                    1ST AD (CONT.)
Roll camera.

                    OPERATOR
    Camera rolling.

                    1ST AD
SOUND?

                    SOUND MIXER
    Speed.

                    1ST AD
    Marker.

The second assistant camera operator comes forward. He holds the clapsticks in front of the camera where the lens is focused.

                    2ND ASST. CAM. OP.
    Scene 27, take one.

He claps the sticks, then dashes back behind the camera.

                    DIRECTOR
    ACTION!

Debby bursts out the door and Newcomer follows. At the door he calls down the hallway.

                    NEWCOMER
    Kathy!

He stops, and looks over at the director. Dropping out of the scene completely.

NEWCOMER

Cut! Cut! I'm sorry, I was supposed to say that further down the hall! I can't believe I did that. I'm sorry!

DIRECTOR

CUT! CUT IT! It's no good! RESET!

Tony, the director, heads swiftly up the hallway toward Newcomer. Newcomer freezes like a rabbit caught in headlights. Without missing a stride, Tony puts an arm on Newcomer and herds him up the hallway, away from the company.

DIRECTOR

Don't EVER do that again. *You* don't call "cut," *I* do. Understand?

NEWCOMER

(Very subdued) Yes, sir. I'm sorry.

DIRECTOR

The mixer can call cut, the camera operator can call cut, and I can. That's it. *Never* an actor. Not ever! If you make a mistake, just forget about it and keep going. Got it?

NEWCOMER

Yes sir.

DIRECTOR

All right. Now just relax, and let's try it again.

He goes back down the hallway shaking his head. The wind is out of Newcomer's sails. He walks slowly back to his first position.

PETER (V.O.)
Hey, everybody makes mistakes. You can't let it get you down.

Newcomer seems to be in a trance.

PETER (V.O. CONT.)
Focus on the scene. What is your objective? To keep Kathy from leaving, right? How are you going to do that? Focus on that! There's no time for self-pity. Keep going forward. You can do it.

But Newcomer has gone numb. He is quiet as he waits behind the apartment door for his cue. He looks up at Debby.

NEWCOMER
Sorry.

DEBBY
Well, as much as I'd love to help you feel better, I'm leaving you.

This last statement gets Newcomer's attention. He suddenly seems more focused.

1ST AD
QUIET ON THE SET!

The set becomes dead quiet.

1ST AD
ROLL camera.

OPERATOR
Camera rolling.

> 1ST AD

SOUND?

> MIXER

Speed.

> 1ST AD

Marker.

> 2ND ASST. CAM. OP.

Scene 27, Take two.

He claps the sticks.

> DIRECTOR

ACTION!

Once again, Debby throws open the door and heads down the hallway. Newcomer comes out after her. This time he calls out her name at the right spot and stops her right on the mark. They get through the scene without any mishaps.

> DIRECTOR

Cut! We'll go again, right away.

> 1ST AD

Back to number one, please!

The director comes over to Newcomer and Debby.

> DIRECTOR

The scene seems flat. (To Debby) Remember, you want out. You're not going to be swayed. but after he asks for one more chance, take a beat before you tell him no. That will make it

DIRECTOR (CONT.)

seem like you're actually considering changing your mind. It'll add a little uncertainty and tension to the scene.

DEBBY

O.K.

DIRECTOR

(To Newcomer) I don't know. It's just not playing. She means everything to you. You've got to make it more important.

NEWCOMER

More pleading?

DIRECTOR

No. Stronger maybe. Convince her, you know? O.K., let's go again.

He goes back behind camera, as Newcomer and Debby head back to the apartment room.

NEWCOMER

Now I'm confused. I don't know what "stronger" means. I mean I'm not exactly in the power position here.

DEBBY

Yeah. Sometimes I think directors and actors need translators.

NEWCOMER

Right.

They wait behind the door for their cue.

PETER (V.O.)

This is your translator speaking. You're thinking of stronger as angrier. But that's not what he means. When you say "one more chance, that's all I'm asking," you have to *mean* that. You have to convince her that you're going to *change*, that you'll be different from this moment on. By strength, he means sincerity. Lock onto her eyes, and pour the truth into her. The truth that you've gotten the message. That you realize that you've been wrong, and that you have the power to change yourself. When you get to that line, find a stillness in yourself. Don't race and don't plead. What you're really saying underneath the line is, "trust me." Don't think about the camera or your marks. You have to convince her whether there are cameras around, or not. This is between you and her.

1ST AD

QUIET ON THE SET! Roll camera.

OPERATOR

Camera rolling.

1ST AD

SOUND?

MIXER

Speed.

1ST AD

Marker.

2ND ASST. CAM. OP.
Scene 27, take three.

DIRECTOR
ACTION!

Debby comes flying out of the door, with Newcomer in pursuit.

NEWCOMER/DOUG
(Partway down the hall) Kathy!

He stops her close to the mark and turns her.

NEWCOMER/DOUG
(Out of breath) Wait a minute.

(Debby eyes him.)

DEBBY/KATHY
Forget it, Doug. It's over.

Newcomer leans forward, staring directly into her eyes. His voice is intimate but determined. He's not thinking about microphones, lenses, lights or directors. Only the woman in front of him and what he wants from her.

NEWCOMER/DOUG
One more chance, that's all I'm asking.

Debby hesitates, as though she *is* going to change her mind about leaving. She slowly removes his hand from her shoulder.

The Next Shot's In The Glass

> DEBBY/KATHY
> The answer . . . is no.

She turns and heads down the hallway. Newcomer stands for a moment, and then follows her.

> DIRECTOR
> CUT! Print that. Very nice.

> SCRIPT SUPERVISOR
> Circle three. Three's a print.

> DIRECTOR
> Check the gate.

> CAMERA OPERATOR
> Gate's clean.

> NEWCOMER
> What's that about?

> DEBBY
> You know, they check to make sure nothing got into the camera that might have ruined the take.

> NEWCOMER
> Right.

> DIRECTOR
> (To Newcomer) That was it. Nice moment when you leaned in.

DEBBY
Yeah, that really helped me. I almost believed you were going to change.

NEWCOMER
Great!

Newcomer is feeling tremendous relief. He's exhausted and ready to go home. He looks at his watch. It's 8:15 in the morning.

DIRECTOR
All right, let's get another one for safety.

1ST AD
Going again. Back to number one.

Newcomer is confused.

NEWCOMER
If that was a print, why are we doing it again?

DEBBY
Sometimes they want to have two in case something goes wrong in developing the film or something.

They walk back to the apartment room.

NEWCOMER
Boy, I thought this was over.

DEBBY
Oh no. We've still got to do the coverage.

NEWCOMER
Oh right. Overs and close-ups probably.

DEBBY
Probably.

NEWCOMER
But I feel like celebrating. Not like doing the scene again.

DEBBY
I know. But it's real dangerous to let down too soon. There's a lot more to shoot. And of course, as the camera gets closer, the more it's going to count. I mean that moment between us isn't going to play in *this* shot, in the *master*. No way. That'll play in the over or the close-up. So don't celebrate too soon.

NEWCOMER
Yeah, I see what you mean.

1ST AD
QUIET ON THE SET! Roll camera.

They do the scene again. Technically, it goes well.

DIRECTOR
Cut! Good, we can use the exit on that. It's cleaner.

SCRIPT SUPERVISOR
Three and four are prints.

MIXER
Three and four. Got it.

                    DIRECTOR
All right, let's move in.

Grips begin moving light poles, the dolly grip moves the
camera and there is a general bustle of activity. What seemed
like chaos to Newcomer before now appears purposeful.

                    1st AD
(To Newcomer and Debby) You two have about
half an hour. Let Stacey know where you are.
Looks like the next set-up is an over on you,
Debby.

                    DEBBY
O.K., thanks. (To Newcomer) Want some
coffee?
                    Peter (V.O.)
Have juice.

                    NEWCOMER
Maybe some juice.

They go to the craft services cart.

                    DEBBY
You're right.

She pours herself some juice. They sit down.

                    NEWCOMER
So the camera will be over my shoulder
shooting onto you.

                    DEBBY
That's it.

NEWCOMER
This may sound stupid, but which shoulder?

DEBBY
You know, I've never been able to figure that
out. I never know which side of the camera to
look at for a close-up, either.

PETER (V.O.)
Tell her you're going to show her.

NEWCOMER
Well, uh, maybe I could help you.

DEBBY
That'd be great. I'd love to get this stuff straight
once and for all.

PETER (V.O.)
Get a pencil and paper.

NEWCOMER
Have you got a pencil?

DEBBY
Sure do, here you go.

NEWCOMER
Thanks.

He turns his script to a blank page.

DEBBY
This is great. I always wanted to understand
this!

>   NEWCOMER
> Yeah, me too.

>   PETER (V.O.)
> Now you just tell her what I tell you. Here we
> go.

>   NEWCOMER
> (To Debby) O.K., here we go.

He draws two figures with a straight line going through both
heads.

>   NEWCOMER
> O.K., this is us.

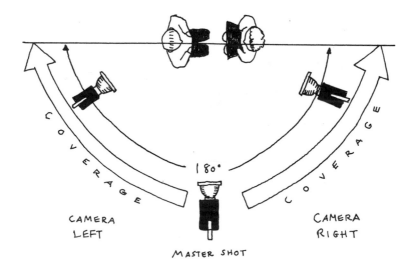

"180° Rule": The master shot defines a 180° semi–circle within which the camera may be
placed to shoot coverage (i.e. 2-shot, OTS, close-up).

DEBBY

Looks like somebody stuck a spear through our heads.

NEWCOMER

It does. Now, remember when we were kids and we dared another kid to cross the line we etched in the dirt with our foot?

DEBBY

Got into a lot of fights with my brother over that.

NEWCOMER

Right. Well, the line going through our heads is the line that the camera cannot cross. If the master is shot from side of that line, then all the rest of the coverage has to be shot from the same side of the line.

DEBBY

Why?

NEWCOMER

Because, if the camera crosses that line and shoots part of the scene from one side, and part of the scene from the other side, the people won't appear to be looking at each other. It will look like they are looking *past* each other. Crossing that line reverses the screen direction.

DEBBY

So, if the master is from one side of that spear through our heads, then the two-shot, overs and close-ups *also* have to be from that same side?

NEWCOMER

Exactly. So, knowing that, you now know which side of camera to look for your fellow actor.

DEBBY

I do?

NEWCOMER

Sure. Look at me.

DEBBY

O.K. (Debby does.)

NEWCOMER

Now, imagine that spear through our heads.

DEBBY

(Laughing) O.K.

NEWCOMER

O.K., that's what they call the *line of axis*.

DEBBY

Fancy.

NEWCOMER

If the camera was on your left, say, when the master was shot . . .

DEBBY

Then it would have to stay on my left for the over and close-up! Right?

NEWCOMER
You got it. It's called the 180° rule.

DEBBY
So when the camera is set up for the over on me, I would know that my look to you would be on the *right* side of the camera.

NEWCOMER
Right. Because that would keep the camera on the correct side of the line.

DEBBY
Which would be on my left side. So, I would take my look to you on the *right* side of the camera in order to keep the camera on my left, which is where it should be in order to preserve the screen direction.

NEWCOMER
Exactly. Now, there are ways to *break* the line of axis, but you won't run into them very often.

DEBBY
Stop! I don't want to know. I think I'll overload. But thanks, that was really helpful.

NEWCOMER
My pleasure.

He turns his script back over and sits back.

DEBBY
Now, if you don't mind, I'm just going to sit quietly for a few minutes and get my brain back

DEBBY (CONT.)
on this scene.

NEWCOMER
Oh, of course. I should do the same.

They both open their scripts and sit quietly.

1ST A.D.
First team please!

DEBBY
That's us.

They go to their marks after their stand-ins have stepped out.

PETER (V.O.)
You did good with that 180° rule stuff. I'm proud of you. Now, line up a near and a far object so that you can find this mark again easily. They're going to want you to step into the shot.

From his position, Newcomer is able to cross-hair a knob on a light pole close to the camera, with the middle of an EXIT sign at the end of the hall. As he is doing this, the focus puller is measuring the distance of Debby's face to the lens, Joel is touching them both up, and a myriad of small lighting adjustments are taking place. He stands still, and lets the crew do their work.

PETER (V.O. CONT.)
You know, a lot of actors fidget while they're trying to line up shots, yakking all the time. I'm glad to see that you know better. Good for you.

PETER (V.O. CONT.)
Now, every set-up has its special requirements.
In an *over*, your responsibility . . .

DIRECTOR
All right, let's see how you get her into this
position.

1ST A.D.
Rehearsal! Quiet!

Newcomer just stands.

DIRECTOR
Newcomer, we need you to *walk into the shot.*
So both of you get out of frame please. (Pause.)
Move out of frame please.

They move.

PETER (V.O.)
They want to be able to cut on *movement,*
because movement on a cut distracts the eye
from the fact that it *is* a cut. Smooth
filmmaking dictates that the cuts be disguised,
if possible. Movement on a cut serves this
purpose.

DIRECTOR
O.K. You're out. Now, swing into it from there.

As Newcomer swings them into the shot, he lines up his
objects.

DIRECTOR

Good. Let's get one. It's quarter to ten and we've only got *two* set-ups!

1ST A.D.

Quiet on the set! We're going right away! 1st positions please.

Newcomer starts back to the apartment room. Debby stops him.

DEBBY

I think he means first positions for *this scene*. You know, where we're just out of frame?

Newcomer stops.

NEWCOMER

Oh, right.

DEBBY

So, it's as if you just caught up and stopped me, and now you're swinging me into this position for the *over*?

NEWCOMER

Right. Got it.

1ST A.D.

ROLL CAMERA.

CAM. OP.

Camera rolling.

1ST A.D.

SOUND?

The Next Shot's In The Glass

MIXER

Speed.

1ST A.D.

Marker.

2ND ASST. CAM. OP.

Scene 27a, take 1.

DIRECTOR

Action.

Newcomer swings Debby into position. He subtly aligns his body with his visual markers, and the scene proceeds. Until . . .

DIRECTOR

CUT IT!

1ST A.D.

That's a cut.

The director walks slowly up to Newcomer.

NEWCOMER

What happened?

DIRECTOR

When you leaned in for that dialogue about asking for one more chance, you blocked her from the camera. But even before the back of your head obliterated her completely, you got in her light, and threw a shadow all over her face.

NEWCOMER

Other than that, how'd you like it? Just kidding.

DIRECTOR

Listen kid, I don't have time for kidding. I'm behind schedule and over budget as it is. Concentrate on what we're doing, and save the jokes. O.K.?

NEWCOMER

O.K. Sorry.

DIRECTOR

Step back in, and we'll show you how much room to move you have before you start shadowing her.

Newcomer goes back to his mark. His face a study in sober concentration.

PETER (V.O.)

That's what I was going to tell you. Your responsibility in an *over* is to make sure the other actor is clear for camera. That means you have to *cheat* your body movements a little. You can't lean quite the same way you did in the master.

CAM. OP.

O.K. lean in please. (Newcomer starts his lean.) Right there is as far *camera right* as you can go.

PETER (V.O.)

Camera right is *your left* as you face the camera. It's the opposite of *stage* right. In this case, since your back is to the camera, *your* right is the same as the *camera's* right.

Newcomer notes how far right he can go without blocking Debby.

> **DIRECTOR**
> Right away.

> **1ST A.D.**
> Quite on the set! First positions, please.

Newcomer and Debby go to their off-camera positions.

> **1ST A.D. (CONT.)**
> ROLL CAMERA.

> **CAM. OP.**
> Camera rolling.

> **1ST A.D.**
> SOUND?

> **MIXER**
> Speed.

> **1ST A.D.**
> Marker.

> **2ND ASST. CAM. OP.**
> Scene 27a, take two.

> **DIRECTOR**
> Action.

Newcomer takes a moment, then swings Debby into the shot at the same speed he did in the master. When he stops, he is in the right position. Everything lines up.

NEWCOMER/DOUG
Kathy, wait a minute!

DIRECTOR
Cut.

Newcomer looks confused.

DIRECTOR
You've already said "Kathy" at this point. You said it when you were half way down the hall. The dialogue picks up *here* with "Wait a minute."

Newcomer feels like an idiot.

NEWCOMER
Right.

DIRECTOR
Let's go again. The energy was good though, keep it up.

He points to the 1st AD.

1ST A.D.
Quiet on the set! Roll camera.

CAM. OP.
Rolling.

1ST A.D.
Sound?

MIXER

Speed.

1ST A.D.

Marker.

2ND ASST. CAM. OP.
Scene 27a, take three. (He claps the sticks.)

DIRECTOR

Action.

Newcomer hits his mark perfectly and begins his dialogue.

NEWCOMER/DOUG
Wait a minute!

DEBBY/KATHY
Forget it Doug. It's over.

Newcomer leans in, but this time just the right amount.

NEWCOMER/DOUG
One more chance. That's all I'm asking.

Debby/Kathy looks uncertainly into his eyes. maybe she'll give him that chance, and maybe she won't. Her hand removes his from her shoulder.

DEBBY/KATHY
The answer . . . is no.

She continues down the hall and out of the shot. Newcomer looks after her, and then follows.

DIRECTOR

Cut, and print it.

SCRIPT SUPERVISOR

Three's the print.

DIRECTOR

Debby, that indecision just plays beautifully.
Makes leaving even stronger.

DEBBY

Thanks. Felt good.

DIRECTOR

All right, let's push in for her close-up.

1ST A.D.

(To Debby) Step in for a line up please.

Kathy steps on her mark.

DEBBY

Which side of camera will I look for Doug?
Wait, don't tell me.

As she thinks, the focus puller runs a tape measure from the
camera to her face, and the electricians refocus the lights.

PETER (V.O.)

You may be wondering why your over isn't the
next set-up. It's because they're already lit in this
direction, so it saves time to push in for this
shot.

DEBBY

I look camera *right* for him, right?

CAM. OP.

Right as can be.

DEBBY

Wow, that is cool. I finally know.

1ST A.D.

(To Newcomer) You're off camera for this one.
Tuck in as close to the lens as you can, so we get
as much of her face on camera as possible.

Newcomer positions himself on the right side of the camera as
near to the lens as he can. It's an uncomfortably tight squeeze.

CAM. OP.

(To Debby) Take your look to Doug please.
(Debby looks at Newcomer.) Looks good.

DIRECTOR

O.K., let's do it.

Joel is madly touching up Debby's make-up.

1ST A.D.

Clear please, Joel.

JOEL

She's shiny. (He finishes powdering.) There.
(He leaves.)

1ST A.D.

Thank you, Joel. Quiet on the set!

PETER (V.O.)
You're probably wondering why she doesn't have to *move* into *this* shot. Right?

1ST A.D.
Roll camera.

CAM. OP.
Camera rolling.

PETER (V.O.)
It's because the change in distance between an over and a close-up is small enough, that it isn't usually disturbing. Some directors still might want her to step into a shot like this, though.

1ST A.D.
Sound?

MIXER
Speed.

1ST A.D.
Marker.

2ND ASST. CAM. OP.
Scene 27b, take one.

He claps the sticks only a few inches from Debby's face.

DIRECTOR
Action.

Off-camera, Newcomer begins his dialogue.

> NEWCOMER/DOUG

Wait a minute.

Newcomer breaks out of character.

> NEWCOMER/DOUG

Oh, sorry. My hand should be on her shoulder.

> DIRECTOR

CUT! Damn it, man! WE DON'T *SEE* YOUR HAND IN THIS SHOT. RIGHT AWAY PLEASE!

Newcomer's confidence is beginning to shatter.

> 1ST A.D.

Quiet on the set. Roll camera.

> CAM. OP.

Camera rolling.

> 1ST A.D.

Sound?

> MIXER

Speed.

> 1ST A.D.

Marker.

> 2ND ASST. CAM. OP.

Scene 27b, take two.

> DIRECTOR

Action.

They play the scene, and all goes well. Newcomer is subdued, Debby happy.

> DIRECTOR
> Very nice. Let's get another.

He goes to Debby.

> DIRECTOR
> Hold that look on Doug a beat or two longer.

> DEBBY
> All right.

The next take is a smooth one.

> DIRECTOR
> Print two and three. All right, let's turn it around.

> 1ST A.D.
> Moving to the other side.

There is a great burst of activity as the camera, lights, cables, sound mixer's cart, craft services cart, people and chairs are moved from one side of the hallway to the other.

> 1st AD
> (To the actors) You've got a few minutes before rehearsal. This'll be coverage on you, Newcomer.

> NEWCOMER
> O.K. So, that means a matching over and a matching close-up?

1ST AD

You got it. Now, you ought to head over to make-up for a touch up.

NEWCOMER

All right.

Newcomer walks out of the apartment building and towards the make-up trailer. At his side walks Peter.

PETER

Well, you did pretty good in there.

NEWCOMER

No, I didn't. I did pretty bad in there is what I did.

PETER

Uh oh.

NEWCOMER

With all that preparation you gave me, I still screwed up.

PETER

Hey, there's a limit to how prepared a person can *be* in one day. Give yourself a break.

NEWCOMER

If I were any good at this, I would just *know* what to do. I would have a feel for it. Let's face it, I'm not cut out for this.

Newcomer opens the door to the make-up trailer and goes in. Peter disappears.

JOEL

Have a seat. (Without a word, Newcomer sits on a make-up chair.) Look up please. (Newcomer does.) Why so quiet? (Newcomer shrugs.) Keeping your energy for the scene. That's smart. It's such an intense scene. The way you do that lean and lower your voice, it adds so much to the tension.

NEWCOMER

You think?

JOEL

Oh, definitely. You can feel it in the room. There, that should do it. I'll take another look right before we shoot.

NEWCOMER

Thanks.

Newcomer leaves the trailer and heads back to the set. He expects to see Peter, but doesn't. At the set, everything is turned around, so that his side of the hallway is clear of any trace of a film company. He finds the craft services cart and pours himself some orange juice.

1ST A.D.

All right, let's get a rehearsal. Newcomer and Debby?

2ND A.D.

They're on set.

1ST A.D.

O.K. 1st team please, for a rehearsal.

Debby and Newcomer come over.

> DIRECTOR
> Newcomer, let's see you turn her into position.

Newcomer does so at performance speed.

> DIRECTOR
> Good. Mark them please.

The second assistant camera operator puts down the marks.

> 1ST A.D.
> Stay there for a minute please.

The first assistant camera operator measures the distance from the camera to Newcomer's face.

> 1ST ASST. CAM. OP.
> You lean in at some point don't you?

> NEWCOMER
> Yes. When I say "one more chance, that's all I'm asking."

> 1ST ASST. CAM. OP.
> Could you show me the lean, please? (Newcomer leans in.) That's as far as you go?

> NEWCOMER
> Yes.

The 1st assistant measures this new distance from the camera to Newcomer's face.

> 1ST ASST. CAM. OP.

Thank you.

> CAM. OP.

Debby, you're blocking him a little. Could you move camera right about two inches?

> DEBBY

Sure. (She does.)

> CAM. OP.

That's good, there.

> DIRECTOR

All right, Newcomer, you're going to swing into the shot. Rehearsal.

> 1ST A.D.

Quiet on the set! Rehearsal.

> DIRECTOR

And . . . action!

Newcomer swings into the shot but misses the mark.

> DIRECTOR

You're off the mark.

Newcomer takes a second and lines up a near and far object.

> DIRECTOR

You don't have to start from so far off, either. Plant your feet, and then lean out of frame. That way you can come into frame almost in position.

NEWCOMER
Good idea. Thanks.

DIRECTOR
A tip I picked up from an old actor. Oh, and
Newcomer, if Debby drifts a little too much
into frame, counter a little camera left.
Remember, if you can see the lens, the lens can
see you. Let's get it lit!

1ST A.D.
2nd team, please!

The stand-ins take their positions on Newcomer and Debby's
marks. Newcomer sits down across from Debby.

DEBBY
So, how're you holding up?

NEWCOMER
Pretty well, I guess. A little nervous.

DEBBY
Yeah, when the camera's on you, the adrenaline
kicks up. You're going to do great. This is a
good scene.

NEWCOMER
Let's hope.

DEBBY
Just forget about the camera, the lights, the
director. This is between us, whether *they're* here
or not.

> 1ST A.D.

First team!

> NEWCOMER

You're right. Thanks.

Newcomer feels excited and ready as they step in.

> DIRECTOR

Let's get a rehearsal, please.

The 1st AD takes the director aside. They seem to be having a serious chat. After a few minutes, they come back.

> DIRECTOR

We'll get this rehearsal and then break for lunch. Let's go!

> NEWCOMER

What?

> DEBBY

I guess they have to, or they'll run into a penalty.

> 1ST A.D.

First positions, please!

They go to their marks. Newcomer lines up a near and a far object almost without thinking about it.

> NEWCOMER

So, we have to wait until after lunch?

DEBBY
Afraid so.

1ST A.D.
Back to number one, please.

They exit the shot so that they can move into it.

DIRECTOR
Action!

Newcomer/Doug stops Debby/Kathy and again swings her into position. They go through the scene.

DIRECTOR
Good. How was it for camera?

CAM. OP.
Fine.

DIRECTOR
O.K., we'll come back to these positions after lunch.

1ST A.D.
LUNCH! ONE HOUR!

Newcomer watches as everyone heads out of the building.

NEWCOMER
(Under his breath) Filmus interruptus.

Debby comes over.

> DEBBY
>
> Come on, let's eat.

They walk out together.

Outside, tables and chairs are set up and people wait in line beside a lunch truck. Newcomer can't believe that just a moment ago he was about to shoot his over and close-up, and now must wait an hour.

> NEWCOMER
>
> This is unbelievable. Why do we have to stop now?

> DEBBY
>
> Union rules. After a certain number of hours, we have to be fed.

They head for the line.

> DEBBIE
>
> Let the crew go first. They really only have *half* an hour.

> NEWCOMER
>
> Oh.

They take trays and get into the line after the crew.

> GRIP
>
> Oh, you can go ahead of us. You're the first shot up after lunch.

DEBBY

Thanks! Come on.

They go to the front. Debby takes everything in sight.

DEBBY

Don't you do what I'm doing. *My* coverage is over. You should eat lightly, otherwise you'll get sleepy and want to crash.

Newcomer takes very little.

NEWCOMER

My stomach's too churned up to eat much anyway.

DEBBY

I know what you mean.

They sit near the camera operator and the Director of Photography. The two of them are poring over a trade catalogue full of new cameras, lenses and lighting instruments. Tech talk abounds.

DEBBY

Boy, that's a whole world I know nothing about.

NEWCOMER

Me neither.

DEBBY

Don't know too much about you either.

NEWCOMER
Well, what do you want to know?

DEBBY
Well, you're a puzzle. Sometimes you seem like you're a real experienced film actor, and other times you seem like a rookie.

NEWCOMER
Yeah.

DEBBY
So, which is it? Are you a rookie, or a veteran?

NEWCOMER
Closer to a rookie than anything. My background is really the theater.

DEBBY
Oh, I'd love to try that sometime, but I'm too scared.

NEWCOMER
Scared?

DEBBY
Yeah, being in front of all those people, going from beginning to end with no retakes. That's scary.

NEWCOMER
That's fun! Nobody can stop you once you get started. You get a long rehearsal period, and people clap when you're done. Paradise!

DEBBY

(Laughing) Well, you make it seem like it's worth trying.

NEWCOMER

Better than this. This is so, well, *scientific*.

DEBBY

True. But you get to work in such detail. That appeals to me. Like, is it more expressive to turn your head this much, or this? Working in such small sections forces you to think about things you might never have.

NEWCOMER

Well, after I got more used to it, maybe it would have its fascinations.

DEBBY

Oh, it would, I'm sure of it.

Newcomer has finished his meager meal. He excuses himself, returns his tray, and walks slowly back to the set. He is expecting Peter to show up. but Peter is not on the set, nor in his head. On the set, crew members are coming back and setting up. Newcomer sits in a cast chair and lets his mind wander. He remembers arriving at the location hours ago feeling lost and inadequate. How innocent he was at 6:15 this morning. Now, he feels like a battle worn veteran. His mind wanders over the scene he is about to shoot. He watches it in his mind's eye. He remembers the excitement of receiving the script at his door, the strange meeting of Peter on the set and in his head, the frozen set, the anger of the director, the elation of having his ideas accepted. He shakes his head. What a day, he thinks.

More and more people are filing in now. Gathering for one purpose. To tell a story the best way they can. What a gift this is, he thinks. All this expense of energy, all this marshaling of forces, not for some act of war, but to serve the imagination. And for a moment, he has his part to play in it. Suddenly Newcomer feels an overwhelming obligation to honor this process, which is so much larger than he; to make his contribution to this extraordinary enterprise. He takes a deep breath, and lets it out.

> 1ST A.D.
> O.K., we're back!

Newcomer comes out of his dream and joins Debby on the set. The director comes over.

> DIRECTOR
> (Clapping his hands) OK! Let's keep the energy up now! First shot after lunch is usually a groggy one! Now, let's get a rehearsal.

> 1ST A.D.
> Quiet on the set! Rehearsing! 1st team, first positions, please.

Newcomer and Debby move a ways off their marks so they can come into the shot.

> DIRECTOR
> Action!

Newcomer finds his mark perfectly.

CAM. OP.
Cut it. She's blocking him.

DIRECTOR
Cut. Give her a better position.

DEBBY
Sorry.

NEWCOMER
Hey, these things happen.

CAM. OP.
Lean your head two inches camera left. (She does.) That's good, there.

DEBBY
Got it. Thanks.

DIRECTOR
Let's save some time and shoot the rehearsal.

1ST A.D.
Back to one, please. This is the Abby Singer!

NEWCOMER
(To Debby) The what?

DEBBY
The Abby Singer. It means the shot before the last shot. Named after a man who used to say it was the last shot, when it wasn't.

NEWCOMER
So, there's only two more shots and we're done

                    NEWCOMER (CONT.)
with this scene?

                         DEBBY
Guess so.

                       1ST A.D.
Quiet on the set! Roll camera.

                       CAM. OP.
Camera rolling.

                       1ST A.D.
Sound?

                        MIXER
Speed.

                       1ST A.D.
Marker.

                  2ND ASST. CAM. OP.
Scene 27c, take one.

He claps the sticks, and hurries out of the shot. Newcomer's
heart is racing. This is his coverage now. Everyone is staring at
him, and every*thing* is pointing at him. He takes a deep breath.

                       DIRECTOR
Action!

Newcomer swings Debby into position, making sure that his
near and far objects are lined up.

                   NEWCOMER/DOUG
Wait a minute.

She stares angrily at him. Newcomer notices that her head is drifting too far into the frame, so he adjusts his head a bit so he can see the full lens with his peripheral vision. He wonders if the scene will be cut, but goes on anyway.

> DEBBY/KATHY
> Forget it, Doug. It's over.

This time, Debby/Kathy starts to move away after the line. She never did that before. Newcomer leans in and speaks with urgency and intensity. He is alarmed that Debby is trying to wreck his over by moving out of the shot. It's as if he is saying to Debby, "Don't do this to me." Suddenly the scene isn't about Doug and Kathy any more, but about Newcomer and Debby.

> NEWCOMER/DOUG
> One more chance. That's all I'm asking.

Debby stares at him, caught up in the urgency. She seems a little frightened of him. After a moment, she removes his arm from her shoulder.

> DEBBY/KATHY
> The answer . . . is no.

She turns and walks a few steps out of frame. That's all the room she has. Newcomer continues to watch her as if she were still walking down the hallway. Why did she do something she had never done in the scene before? Was she trying to throw him? He feels betrayed, angry and hurt all at once. After a few moments, he goes after her.

> DIRECTOR
> Cut! (To Newcomer) So, you've been saving all
> the good stuff for your coverage, huh? That was

DIRECTOR (CONT.)
terrific! Print it!

SCRIPT SUPERVISOR
Print on one.

DIRECTOR
(To Newcomer) I think you're going to be real happy with that. (To the 1st AD) Let's push in for the close-up.

1ST A.D.
(To Newcomer) Would you stand on your mark please?

Newcomer goes to his mark. He is confused. The director loved what he did, but he wasn't playing the scene. He wasn't acting. he let his true feelings about the *actress* come out, not his reactions to the *character*. That can't be right, can it? That's not acting. And why did Debby *do* that to him? Lost in thought, he doesn't see that Debby has come over to him.

DEBBY
That take was really good. It had so much in it.

NEWCOMER
Thanks. Debby why did you start to pull away like that when you said it was over?

DEBBY
Yeah, sorry. I don't know. It felt right, somehow. And as I was doing it I realized what you must be thinking, and I thought if you stayed with it and didn't get thrown, that it might serve the scene really well. And it did. You did great!

NEWCOMER
Well, I'll tell you, I was really mad about it. I thought you were trying to sabotage my scene or something.

DEBBY
No, no. I wouldn't do that to you, or anybody. But sometimes adding a new element into a scene that you've shot over and over again, can spice it up, bring it back to life.

NEWCOMER
Well, I guess it worked. Thanks, I think.

Debby laughs.

1ST A.D.
We're ready.

DIRECTOR
Let's shoot it!

1ST A.D.
Quiet on the set! The next shot's in the glass!

The crew gives out some shouts of approval.

NEWCOMER
(To Debby, who is positioned close by and next to the camera lens) Now, what's *that* mean?

DEBBY
You got me. Never heard that one before.

CAM. OP.
It means this is the last shot here. The next one

CAM. OP. (CONT.)
will be the liquid of your choice in a cocktail glass.

NEWCOMER
(Smiling) I see.

1ST A.D.
Roll camera.

CAM. OP.
Camera rolling.

1ST A.D.
Sound?

MIXER
Speed.

1ST A.D.
Marker.

2ND ASST. CAM. OP.
Scene 27d, take one.

DIRECTOR
Action!

Newcomer is suddenly confused. He isn't sure if he is supposed to move into this shot, or begin on his mark. he isn't even sure which part of the dialogue he should start with.

DIRECTOR
Cut! Is there a problem?

NEWCOMER
I'm sorry. Do I come into this shot or do I start

NEWCOMER (CONT.)
from here?

DIRECTOR
Good question. You can lean into frame, as if you've just turned her around. And start with "wait a minute." Try the move for camera.

Newcomer leans out of the frame.

CAM. OP.
O.K., lean back in . . . Good, right there.

1ST A.D.
Right away. Quiet on the set! Roll camera.

CAM. OP.
Lean back out, Newcomer. (He does.) Camera rolling.

1ST A.D.
Sound?

MIXER
Speed.

1ST A.D.
Marker.

2ND ASST. CAM. OP.
Scene 27d, take two.

He claps the sticks and moves out of the shot.

DIRECTOR
Action.

Newcomer leans into the shot, his arm reaching out of frame as if he has his hand on Debby/Kathy's shoulder. In reality, she is too far away, but in the lens, this *cheat* looks good.

> NEWCOMER/DOUG
> Wait a minute.

Out of the corner of his eye, Newcomer notices the script supervisor talking earnestly with the director.

> DEBBY/KATHY
> Forget it, Doug. It's over.

> NEWCOMER/DOUG
> One more chance . . .

> DIRECTOR
> Cut! Newcomer, you're using the wrong hand. The *other* one was on her shoulder in all the other shots.
> Newcomer looks at his outstretched arm.

> NEWCOMER
> You're right. I'm sorry, I don't know how that happened.

> DEBBY
> Don't worry. These things happen.

> DIRECTOR
> The energy was a little low as well. All right let's go again.

> 1ST A.D.
> Right away. Back to one. (Newcomer leans out of the shot.) ROLL CAMERA.

CAM. OP.

Camera rolling.

1ST A.D.

SOUND?

MIXER

Speed.

1ST A.D.

Marker.

2ND ASST. CAM. OP.

Scene 27d, take three.

DIRECTOR

Action!

Newcomer leans into the shot with more energy, and with the correct arm outstretched.

NEWCOMER/DOUG

Wait a minute!

DEBBY/KATHY

Forget it Doug, it's . . .

But before she can finish the line, Newcomer, with his newfound energy, cuts in with *his* line, talking over her.

NEWCOMER

One more chance, that's . . .

He doesn't get much further.

> DIRECTOR
CUT!

Everything stops. The director walks over to Newcomer, throws an arm around his shoulder, and they take their second excursion up the hallway.

> DIRECTOR
In a close-up, Newcomer, do *not* overlap dialogue unless you're told that it's all right to do so.

> NEWCOMER
I'm sorry, but I don't know what you mean by the term "overlapping."

> DIRECTOR
I see.

He takes a deep breath.

> DIRECTOR
Well, overlapping means talking at the same time as someone else. If the scene requires you to overlap the other character's dialogue, you can do it in the master, or in any of the other coverage, *but not the close-up.*

> NEWCOMER
Why not?

> DIRECTOR
You know, I'm behind schedule on this project, and today has not been the smoothest of days, but I'm going to take the time to tell you anyway.

NEWCOMER

No, you really don't have to. I'm really starting
to feel guilty.

DIRECTOR

It's not your fault. They've given me an
impossible schedule. I'm going to need another
week to finish. But I don't feel guilty. It takes
the time that it takes. That's all. We do the best
we can with the limitations we're given.
Anyway, if part of Debby's dialogue is on your
close-up, then I'm married to it. Suppose I want
to put some space between what you say and
what she says. I can't control that if part of her
dialogue is on your shot. See?

NEWCOMER

Kind of.

DIRECTOR

Well, that's good enough for now. You should
come into the editing room sometime. I'll show
you. But now, we gotta get back to work.

They walk back to the set.

DIRECTOR

Let's shoot it.

The crew snaps back like a rubber band. Everyone is ready.

1ST A.D.

(To Newcomer) Step in, please. (He does.)
Quiet on the set? Roll camera.

CAM. OP.
Camera rolling.

1ST A.D.
Sound?

MIXER
Speed.

1ST A.D.
Marker.

2ND ASST. CAM. OP.
Scene 27d, take four.

DIRECTOR
Keep up the intensity. Remember you want her
back. No overlaps, and . . . action!

Newcomer leans into the frame. He looks focused and
determined.

NEWCOMER/DOUG
Wait a minute.

Debby gives him a look of disdain from off camera.

DEBBY/KATHY
Forget it, *Doug*. It's over.

Anger flashes across Newcomer's face at the sarcastic way she
has said his name. He instantly covers it over.

NEWCOMER/DOUG
One more chance, that's all I'm asking.

He is strong and steady now. Debby takes a long time before she replies. Off camera she mimes removing his hand from her shoulder, and on camera, Newcomer reacts.

> DEBBY
> (Removing the hand) The answer . . . is no.

Instead of turning to leave right away, she holds a look with him. He reacts. After a few moments, she turns her back to him as if she is heading down the hallway and out of the building. He follows her with his eyes, careful not to look too far off camera. After a beat, he leaves frame to go after her.

> DIRECTOR
> Cut it, and print it! We're out of here.

> SCRIPT SUPERVISOR
> Print four.

The director walks over to Newcomer.

> DIRECTOR
> Nice job.

> NEWCOMER
> Thanks. And thank you for your patience.

> DIRECTOR
> Hey, thanks for giving me a chance to *be* patient. It's not usually a part of my job description. See you next week for scene 26.

> NEWCOMER
> Right. See you.

He gets no final good-bye because the director is moving to a new location for the rest of the day's shoot.

> **1ST A.D.**
> O.K., Newcomer, you're wrapped for today. Stacey will sign you out at your trailer after you change.

> **NEWCOMER**
> All right, thanks.

> **1ST A.D.**
> You bet. We'll call you about next week.

> **NEWCOMER**
> O.K.

The 1st leaves. Newcomer looks back at the hallway that has been the scene of his filmic baptism. Only a few cables remain as evidence of what took place here. The company has moved on. Newcomer feels strange. So much has happened, and yet he has a feeling of anticlimax. He's finished, and yet there's no sense of completion. Shouldn't there be a celebration, some moment to mark this milestone? Of course there should be, he thinks. There just isn't any time for it. What a funny business. So much concern and focus directed at you and then total abandonment. Put away until the next time. "Wrapped." You move, with no transition, from the center of the picture to the margin. Well, he thinks, it's not so different from life. You're here for a while, and then, you're gone. The real reward is in the doing. He turns around and heads out of the building.

After retrieving his wallet from the prop people, he goes to his trailer and changes. There is a knock at his door.

NEWCOMER

Come in.

The door opens.

PETER

Hiya, kid.

Newcomer is startled.

NEWCOMER

Peter. Hey, what happened to you? You just
disappeared. Left me out there by myself! Right
when I needed you the most!

PETER

I'm not a nursemaid. Besides, you did pretty
well without me.

NEWCOMER

Whoever you are.

PETER

Still trying to figure it out, eh?

NEWCOMER

So?

PETER

Take it easy. I'm not making fun. Look I just
stopped by to tell you that you did a good job
out there.

NEWCOMER

Thanks.

PETER

And that when the 2nd AD comes to sign you out, make sure that the times she has down for you are written in ink. Some unscrupulous companies put them in pencil and then after you've gone, erase them and put in new ones.

NEWCOMER

What for?

PETER

To save on any overtime or meal penalties.

NEWCOMER

What's a meal penalty?

PETER

Ask your agent. Also, keep a log of your work hours. Start it right now. When you were called, when you got to the location, when you began shooting, when you ate, and when you signed out. Well, that's about it. See you around sometime.

NEWCOMER

Wait a minute! Don't I get an explanation?

Peter goes to the trailer door.

PETER

Sorry, I got stuff to do.

He opens the door to go out.

NEWCOMER

Wait a second! I owe you a lot, and I want to thank you.

PETER

Hey, Newcomer, *I* didn't do anything. *YOU* did.

He leaves.

Chapter   7

Tell Me The Story Up To Here

In his book *Film Technique and Film Acting*, the great Russian director and pupil of Lev Kuleshov, Vsevolod Pudovkin, defined the task of the film actor as "creating the illusion of a continuous performance." "Illusion," because the process of filmmaking is such a *dis*continuous and fragmented one. In addition to the problem of shooting individual scenes over and over again from different angles, the actor is also faced with the obstacle of shooting scenes *out of order.* An actor may shoot a scene from the middle of the film one day, a scene from the ending in the next week, and a scene from the beginning, in the next month.

Complicating this is the fact that the audience must *never be aware* that the scenes following each other seamlessly on screen were shot weeks or months apart and out of sequential order. If a character is outside of a building arguing with his friend, and then enters the interior of the building, the actor must make it appear as though all of this is unfolding in real time. Even though the interior might have been shot first, and the outside scene weeks later, the actor must make it *seem* as though it happened as it looks on screen.

Is there a method to this madness? Why aren't films and episodic television shows shot *in sequence?* Sometimes they are. If a film takes place in only one location, the filmmakers will make an attempt to shoot it in order. In Robert Altman's *McCabe and Mrs. Miller*, an entire town was constructed in a single location. This allowed the filmmaker to shoot in scenic order. Or if a major character must undergo significant physical change during the course of a film, the shooting order may be designed to follow that change. In *Philadelphia*, Tom Hanks' character must be seen to physically waste away over the course of the film. In order to show this, scenes were shot as close to their consecutive order as possible.

Actors working in four camera television situation comedies also avoid the out of order problem. These shows, wherein multiple points of view are shot by four cameras simultaneously, are performed from beginning to end. This is desirable because they are usually shot before an audience, and possible because they are performed on one of several sets lined up next to each other (mirroring, in a way, the *polyscenic stage of juxtaposition* of the Medieval theater). When the actors finish a scene on one set, they walk over to the next set for the next scene and play it there from beginning to end. This requires all four cameras to be on one side of the line of axis for shooting simultaneous coverage.

Instead of shooting a master and then relighting and repositioning for coverage, as is done for one-camera film and episodic television, the director can let the actors go from beginning to end knowing that all the different kinds of shots will be recorded at the same time. There is a steep price to pay, however, for this convenience. The production is limited to the confines of a sound stage, and camera movement is severely limited. For the actor, however, shooting in order this way is much closer to performing in the theater: You begin at the beginning and end at the ending.

But aside from these examples, the vast majority of film and episodic television shows are shot *out* of sequence. Again, we ask why? The answer is simple: Economics.

A day of shooting is one of the most expensive days in the history of the world. The costs of assembling people, equipment and supplies is astronomical. The size of some movie budgets can make one gasp with astonishment. 40 million, 50 million, even 80 million dollars. With expenses like these, it is no wonder that production companies do whatever they can to reduce costs. The more that can be accomplished in a day, the better. So naturally, a system has evolved that uses time as efficiently as possible.

For example, supposing a movie takes place in only two locations. And further, imagine that these two locations are a house and a bank. For this movie, we want to shoot both interiors and exteriors at each location. In this movie, called *Insufficient Funds*, scenes 1, 4, 7, 9, 11, 32-34, and 41 are at the house, and scenes 2-3, 5-6, 8, 10, 12-31, and 35-40 are at the bank. The bank, incidentally, is charging us $2,000 per day for its use. Suppose now, that we want to shoot this film in sequence. Scene one is an exterior of the house, with the main characters swimming in their pool. Fine. We shoot it. Now, for scene two, we must change the actors clothing, move the company to the bank, light, rehearse, and then shoot. Most of the day is now gone. But because we are unusually efficient, we also shoot scene three. The next day, we start back at the house for scene four. All goes well, so by 10:30 a.m. we move back to the bank for scenes five and six. We pay the bank another $2,000, and shoot. These were short scenes, so we head back to the house for scene seven, an interior. We finish at the house by 4:00 pm and decide to try to squeeze in scene eight back at the bank. We don't get a shot though, because by the time we move and set up, we don't have enough time. We wrap for the day tired and exhausted. Trying to shoot in sequence like this is costing us money, time and energy. The title of our film is rapidly becoming our financial reality. So someone suggests that we shoot by *location*. This is a revolutionary idea, but we try it.

We stay at the house for the number of days that it takes to shoot the scenes there, and then move to the bank to shoot all of the scenes that take place *there*. Lo and behold, we are at the bank far fewer days (saving us thousands), and we finish ahead of schedule and under budget. Shooting by location and not by scene order has done the trick. This is the reality that directors and actors must deal with. When it comes to scheduling, their needs are not always paramount. So then, how does the actor keep track of where, in this confusing jig-saw puzzle, he is?

During the shooting of *Gone with the Wind*, Vivien Leigh is said to have asked the director every morning before a scene, "tell me the story up to here." This way, she was able to keep track of what she knew and what *she didn't know*, prior to each scene. This is crucial. It kept her in the present moment, with full understanding of the events that had led *up* to the scene, but no knowledge of what happened *after*. If she had already shot scenes subsequent to the one at hand, she needed to forget them. They had no bearing on the present scene because, as far as the *character* knew, they hadn't happened yet. This way, she guarded herself against playing the future in the present. When actors make this mistake it is called *anticipating*.

Unfortunately, most directors do not have the time to comply with requests like Ms. Leigh's, so the actor must perform this task for himself. It is a very useful idea for each actor in a scene to tell himself the story "up to here," and there are several tools that can help actors do this.

After reading the whole script at least ten times, the actor can remove pages from it and make a second script consisting of only his part. Now, if he reads the script that does *not* contain his part, he can more easily see how his story affects the whole. What effect does it have when his part is removed? Then, reading the script that contains *only* his part gives him a clearer picture of his character's story and development. With such a script, the actor can easily see what happened to him last before a new scene begins. This understanding of the character's *preceding incident* is critical to how the next scene will be played. But this can also be misleading. The actor needs a *third* script to avoid a trap here. Remember, he has one with *only* his part, and one *without* his part. But he also needs a *complete* script. Other characters may talk about him in their scenes and reveal critical information. If the actor looks only at his *character* script, he may easily forget about events that may have happened off screen, or in scenes in which he does not appear but that dramatically affect him. So now the actor has three scripts. A complete one, one with his part removed, and one that contains only his part. Each complements the other, and gives the actor a better grasp of the whole story and his place in it. The next step is to create *timelines*.

Stories usually take place over days, months, or years. Creating a story timeline showing both the actor's scenes and when they take place is invaluable for keeping track of where in story time one is. Such a time line might look like this:

Day 1	Day 2	Day 3	Day 6
Sc. 4-7, 9 11,15	Sc. 27	Sc. 41,45, 47-51 53, 67, 70	Sc. 92,94 101-112

At a glance, the actor knows how every scene he is in fits into the time scale of the story being told. If some scenes are night ones, the actor merely adds these to the time line. If the story takes place in a single day, the actor can make an hour by hour timeline. Timelines should be tailored to the demands of each script.

Unfortunately, this timeline tells the actor nothing about the *shooting* time. For that, another type of timeline and some more information is needed.

During the shooting of a film or television show, the actor is usually only given a day's notice of what scene or scenes he will be shooting. This information is on the call sheet. But to gain some idea of the whole shooting schedule, the actor needs to ask for a *day out of days*. This is a relatively detailed description of what scenes, which actors and what equipment is required for each day of the shoot. A day out of days also lists a title for each scene. This title amounts to the *action* of the scene, and sometimes can serve as the line or scene objective for the actor. It is a good idea for the actor to emulate this, and give a short action title to every scene he is in.

If a day out of days is not available, the actor should then ask for a *one-liner*. This also is a listing of what scenes are scheduled to shoot on what days, but is not nearly so detailed as a day out of days. Remember, these shooting schedules are always being revised. But with the information from these schedules the actor can make a shooting timeline that will keep him prepared. He must understand, though, that he has to keep his timeline up to date or he will get lost.

With a script and some sort of shooting schedule, the actor can make a map of his way through the production. It might look like this:

SHOOTING TIME

Feb.7	Feb. 8	Feb. 12	Feb. 15	Feb. 20
SC. 41, 45 92,94	SC. 4,7,9 101-112	SC. 27, 4-7 11,15	SC. 47-51	SC. 67,70

Since scenes 41 and 45 and 92 and 94 take place at a hospital in our imaginary script, they have been scheduled together. By looking at his *story* time line, the actor can quickly see that two different story days are involved on the February 7th shooting day. Now he can easily see that on this first day of work, he will be dealing with two different wardrobes, different sets of actors, and different story events. This knowledge prepares the actor for the demands of the day, and helps him to concentrate on the work at hand. If he has titled each scene with a short action statement of the line or scene objective, he now has a quick guide through the maze of production. With his scripts, his timelines and his titles, he always knows *where he is* and *what he is doing*. Additional preparation is also helpful. If the part demands many wardrobe or make-up changes, the actor can create a costume and make-up timeline. Keeping timelines and titles together with the character script makes a neat and streamlined package. And while these aids may seem cumbersome, they are, in reality, an actor's lifeline.

I was once cast in a film that featured nearly as many *flashbacks* as real time sequences. Unfortunately, the writer had neglected to identify which scenes were which. So, I first had to go through and determine what was a flashback scene and what wasn't, and then had to create two character scripts. One with only the real time scenes, and one with only the flashback scenes. Then, I had to create timelines for each type of scene so I would not become hopelessly lost. With these timelines, I could quickly determine if the scene coming up was a flashback or a real time one. Without this aid, I would never have made it through. In fact, when I showed these timelines to the director, he used them to keep *him* on track.

Shooting out of sequence is one of the greatest problems that actors face. But if the actor can quickly and easily locate himself in time and space, know where he is and what he is doing, tell himself the "story up to here," he can construct and develop his part with confidence. And if he weds his native talent to his craft, he can play his part so that it unfolds as a growing and continuous whole.

Chapter 8

We'll Fix It In Post

Because the film process is such a complex one, it is usually broken down into three manageable phases. The first is *pre-production*. This part of the process includes finalizing the script, hiring personnel, location scouting, scheduling and budgeting. The next phase is *production*. This involves the actual shooting, directing and acting of the script. When the principal photography of this phase is over, the actor's job is finished. Or is it? Not really. Much to a novice actor's surprise, he has a role to play in the final phase of the filmmaking process known as *post-production*.

In broad terms, post-production involves the editing and assembling of the film into a releasable form. This requires the efforts of picture and sound editors, recordists, composers, film labs, special effects people, post-production supervisors, producers and many others. There is much to do. The film must be printed up, and duplicate negatives made. No changes or cuts are made on the *original* negative until all decisions affecting its final form have been decided and agreed upon. Then, a special negative cutter is hired who conforms the original negative to the agreed upon final version. A temporary sound track is laid in, dialogue re-recorded, effects put in, titles added, a score recorded, a dub stage mix done, an answer print reviewed and approved, and release copies made.

If something has gone wrong during the production phase, producers and directors often hope that corrections can be made by the expertise and manipulations of the post-production team. As they say, "We'll fix it in post." But what has the actor got to do with all this? Wait a minute. Did I say dialogue re-recorded? Indeed I did.

Six months after finishing principal photography on *Car Wash*, I received a call from my agent relaying a request from Universal Studios who had made the film. They wanted to know if I would be free on the upcoming Thursday to "loop" my scenes. I had no idea what to say because I had no idea what "loop" meant. I asked the agent. She said it meant to do some of my dialogue over again on a sound stage. She wasn't sure exactly *how* this was done, or *why*, but assured me that I would be paid a bit extra for my time. So, with a gulp, I agreed to meet at the specified address, and "loop."

When the day came, I was very anxious. Do the dialogue again? Had I been so awful that I had to perform some sort of emergency operation on myself? Should I be ashamed that I had been called in to "loop?" And worst of all, was I going to have to *see* myself? I wasn't ready for that.

When I arrived at the appointed location, I was ushered through a heavy door with a red warning light above it into a small room. Taking up one entire wall of this room was a large screen. Across from it was a control booth isolated from the sound stage by a glass wall. A post-production supervisor came out and introduced himself, explaining that the director couldn't be there. He was going to be my guide. First, he showed me a sheet which contained all of the dialogue I was to re-record. It was nearly every line I had. My heart sank. Didn't I *do* all this six months ago? Why did I have to do it again, I wondered. How was I going to "get into it" again after all this time? There were no other actors to play to; I wasn't in the same location. The whole thing seemed like a cruel joke. How was I going to do this? I didn't *say* any of this, of course.

It was time for my first line. The screen flickered to life, and suddenly there I was. I heard my screen self say the line I was supposed to loop. It was very soft. Too soft.

"See," said the producer, "we need a little more level on that." I nodded my head. He was right. But I was still getting over the shock of seeing myself. After a moment or two, I confessed to him that I had never done this before, and didn't have a clue how to proceed.

"Well," he explained, "some of the lines you're going to do over need to be matched with the movements of your lips. These are called *sync* lines. Other lines we're going to do today are *not* sync lines, and they'll be a lot easier. Now, we're not going to bite off more than we can chew. We'll just go one line at a time. The sound editor has timed out where you begin to speak, with a series of beeps. You'll hear three of them spaced about a second apart. Where the fourth beep would be, that's where you start your line. You can wear headphones if you like and listen to the line as you said it six months ago on the set, or try it *without* listening to it. Up to you."

I had no idea which way I would prefer, so I tried the headphones. They rolled the film back, and the forward again. The beeps beeped, and I waited for my line to come over the headphones. When I heard it, I started. Too late.

"Cut," called the producer. "You have to go by the beeps. If you wait for your voice, you'll be too late. If you wait to see your lips move, that'll also be too late. Believe me, stick with the beeps."

I tried again. No dice.

"Cut," he called. "You clipped the head." I looked at him, puzzled. "Means you came in too soon. Don't worry, it happens to everybody. Just start talking when the fourth beep would sound. Maybe, take off the cans. We'll put the beeps on the horn out here." I correctly guessed that the "cans" were the headphones, and soon realized that the "horn" referred to the speakers in the room. I tried again, and got all the way through the first line.

"You're getting closer," said the producer, but the sync is a little rubbery. "Let's go again." Well, I spent the better part of the day slowly working my way through each line of dialogue. It was difficult work, and scary as well. Much of my vocal performance had now been re-recorded six months after principal photography had been completed. And I found myself worrying more about syncing my lines than performing them. Had I damaged my performance? Why was this process necessary anyway, I wondered again. How often are actors asked to do this? And why hadn't I been warned? It took some time before I realized how important and how large a part looping plays in an actor's life.

Looping, or Automated Dialogue Replacement (ADR), is a part of most film and television made today. There are several reasons for this. The recording of sound is not a perfect process. Microphone batteries get low on power, microphone placement might be misjudged, boom operators make mistakes, recording levels might be incorrectly set, room air conditioners can cause a low level hum on the track, and so on. Shooting exteriors presents even more problems. Car horns, planes overhead, fog horns, barking dogs, industrial noises, all these conspire to ruin the recording of clean dialogue tracks. Because of this, a great deal of dialogue needs to be *re*-recorded.

If a plane flies overhead during one actor's piece of dialogue, the director usually cuts the scene, and the company waits for the sound to die away. But if ambient (background) noises persist, the company must push on and complete the day's work. At this point, the director is telling himself that "we'll fix it in post." But not just one actor's dialogue must be looped. No. Even if the other actor in the scene was recorded cleanly, he too will be called in to loop. This is because the looped lines would not match the levels and background sound of the original production track. Cutting from a looped line back into an original sounds uneven. In addition, the ambient sound of the original location will sound completely different from the ambient sound of the looping stage. Sound technicians try to compensate for this by recording several minutes of *room tone* on the set. This, then, is laid underneath the looped lines so that they blend more naturally with the sound of the location. But even so, a trained ear can almost always detect a looped line. So, an actor may well be called in to loop whose performance is perfect and whose dialogue is cleanly recorded.

Sometimes a producer or the director finds it necessary to rewrite a scene after it has been shot. This, of course, is only possible in post-production. Sometimes the need is for lines to be added, and sometimes for lines to be changed. This usually has little to do with the excellence of the actor's original performance. The producers or director have found a flaw in the writing or construction of the scene, and are simply trying to correct it. But sometimes, the reason for looping is what the actor fears. Parts of his performance have been found wanting.

An actor can look at looping in two ways. He can dread the

process and defend his original choices, or he can, as Orson Wells and Dustin Hoffman have pointed out, see the process as an opportunity to improve his performance. Even if a loop exists because of a technical glitch, the actor may as well take the opportunity to try and improve what is there. If what is there *needs* no improvement, the actor must try to do it again. Getting into a scene months after it is over is not easy. And yet, it is amazing how quickly the feeling of the set, the people and the emotions, comes back. The actor needs to remind himself of what he wants in the scene, what's in his way, how he gets it, and how he feels about winning or losing. Producers and actors sometimes disagree about the interpretation of a character or moment. When this happens, the actor must make his point clearly and forcefully. The producer or director may be persuaded. But if not, the actor's job is to try his best to give what is asked of him.

A healthy respect for the looping process will help an actor to get through it successfully. It can even be fun. The anonymity of the looping stage can be freeing. No cameras are pointing. No one is staring at you. Without the endless distractions of the set you can concentrate in relative peace. It doesn't happen often in life, but in looping, the actor truly gets a try at a Second Chance.

Chapter 9

The Interactive Actor

In some ways, the history of film and television can be seen as the quest on the part of filmmakers to gain greater control over the elements of production. Loss of light, intrusive noise and unpredictable weather conditions led to the creation of the *sound stage*. Greater microphone and film stock sensitivities, better film projection systems, more maneuverable cameras, more sensitive lenses, and improved lighting and sound technologies have given filmmakers more control over what can be filmed and how. But some elements in the production chain have resolutely refused to be controlled or improved. The people.

Writers still don't meet deadlines. Directors still have "creative differences," and actors still won't come out of their trailers. What's to be done? In the case of the actor, new technologies are challenging his historic uncontrollability.

With today's digital technologies, it is possible to exercise a good deal of control over both the actor's recorded voice and his recorded image. If an actor today takes a bit too much time doing a thirty second *voice over*, the editors can digitally compress the voice track to fit into whatever time frame they want. And this is done *without distorting the sound of the voice*.

The Interactive Actor

It used to be that if a recorded voice was speeded up, the pitch of that voice would rise. Alvin and the Chipmunks were the result of this process. But today a voice can be made to fit a space of time without altering the sound of the voice at all. So an actor's timing can be manipulated in post-production to a greater degree than ever before. It is even possible today to digitally sample an actor's voice, and then have that voice enunciate dialogue that the actor never spoke. Actors have always feared losing their voices, but never in this particular way. So, the actor's voice is manipulatable. What about his body?

In 1988, the movie *Willow* introduced a new special effect called *morphing*. With this technique, it became possible to transform one shape seamlessly into another. In 1991, this effect gained world wide notoriety because of its use in the very popular Arnold Schwarzenegger vehicle *Terminator 2*. By 1993, this technology became available to the home computer user for the affordable price of $150.00. So, it is now possible to sample a voice, digitize a body image, and create an ersatz actor on a computer. An actor totally controllable by the user.

Today, computer programmers can create convincing images of human beings with the new technology. In the movie *The Babe,* 1000 extras were turned into 20,000 screaming baseball fans, using sampled and digitized people. These digitized human images are now being used not only for extras, but also for stunt work. Why endanger a human being when a computer simulation can take the punishment risk free? Perhaps in the future someone will create a digital actor or actress whose popularity will rival the stars of today. More likely than being *replaced* by the new technologies, however, is the likelihood that actors will have to learn new ways to work *with* them.

Today, and in the near future, actors will find themselves working increasingly on *blue screen* sound stages. These are stages hung with a large blue (sometimes green) backdrop. This is nothing unusual, of course. Movies and television shows have shot with rear screen projection for many years. What *is* new, however, is the way the blue screen is being used. In this new process, called the *ultimatte* process, both the background and the foreground are processed, combined and digitally manipulated. The result is so convincing that it becomes virtually impossible to tell that John Lithgow is *not* standing on that mountain in the film *Cliffhanger*, or that the President of the United States in the film *In the Line of Fire* is *not* standing before cheering crowds, or that in the movie *Forrest Gump*, Tom Hanks is *not* really seeing some of the figures he is talking with. In all of these cases, the actors did their scenes on a sound stage in front of a blue screen which to them appears blank. For actors, this is a difficult way to work. One of the factors that affects a character's behavior is where they are. One acts differently in a throne room than one does on a mountain top. The actor must get as precise an explanation of the "where" of his scene as he can when working on a blue screen set. And even then his imagination must work overtime to create that unseen reality. Acting to, or with, something that isn't there is a difficult problem for an actor to overcome. The problem is compounded when the "who" of a scene is absent as well, as in the films *Roger Rabbit* and *Forrest Gump*.

In the film *The Entity*, the director asked me one day to react to the supernatural force that was the namesake of the movie. None of us knew what this force looked like, so I asked the director. He said he didn't know. He said he hadn't liked any of the effects he'd been shown so far, and consequently had no idea what the "entity" looked like. I was stumped. I still needed to know how to react to it. Was it scary? Was it benign looking? What? Again, he said he didn't know. Suddenly, the camera was rolling and I had to do something. I looked off in the distance at a blank wall, drew in a breath, and put a startled and fearful look on my face. Months later at a test screening, I was told that at that tense moment in the film the audience had burst out laughing. It turned out that the final approved effect was a kind of cute green blob that wouldn't have frightened a mouse. My reaction looked ridiculous, and was mercifully cut from the film. What should I have done?

When acting with special effects that are going to be put in after principal photography has been completed, it is a good idea to remember the Kuleshov effect. If I had had an intense but largely enigmatic and non-committal expression on my face, the audience could have read onto it an appropriate reaction. If the apparition *had* been a gruesome one, I would have seemed paralyzed with fear. If, as was the case in *The Entity*, the effect looked *non*-threatening, I would have seemed fascinated by the strangeness before me. In either case, *underplaying* the moment would have been my safest and probably most effective choice.

The new technologies do not present only difficulties to the actor, however. They also present opportunities. New jobs and new challenges are invigorating the field as never before.

The computer video game, *Betrayal at Krondor* boasts in its advertising that it contains over 2500 frames of *rotoscoped* animation. The rotoscope process involves actors. Years ago, when Walt Disney and other animators were searching for ways to make their productions more realistic, they hit upon the process of rotoscoping. In this process, real actors, in full costume, are filmed acting the scenes later intended for animation. This film is then projected onto a large white surface frame by frame. The animator can then draw the outlines of the movements of the actors and the clothing, and more accurately depict real life motion. This was done for many of the Disney Company's full scale productions such as *Sleeping Beauty* and *Cinderella*. Today, rotoscoping is being used by video game makers such as Lucas Arts, Sierra Dynamix and others. But the area of new technology which may have the greatest impact on actors and how they do their work is the area of *interactive multimedia*.

When a film or CD-ROM disk is interactive, it means that the audience must come up with seven different endings to his story, the interactive director must plan and shoot seven different plausible endings, and the interactive actor must be able to believably act seven different endings. Of course, interactive movies and CD-ROMs will feature many more intervention points than just one. A recent interactive movie shown in New York provided over *sixty* places for audience intervention.

For the many creative artists involved, this presents a new way of working. In an interactive movie, the actor must keep track of each different story line so that each one seems logical and continuous. This is a greater problem even than shooting out of order. A good way to keep all the alternate story lines distinct is to create a different script for each. Telling oneself "the story up to here" will be multiplied by the number of story alternatives written into the script. This way of working also places new demands on the actor's range. In a single interactive movie, the actor's character may turn out to be the villain in one story alternative, the hero in another, the lover in another, the beggar in another. He may be required to show tenderness in one scenario, callousness in another, fear in another, rage in another, and tears in another. The possibilities are limited only by the imagination of the writer.

In some cases, the new technologies combine to create a new

working environment. In the interactive CD-ROM movie *Voyeur*, produced by Phillips Interactive Media, many of the scenes were shot against a blue screen. So in addition to acting alternate scenarios, the actor is faced with imagining the environment as well. To help the actor, monitors can be set up off screen which show the computer-generated background. This helps the actor to see the "where" in which he is acting. This requires the actor to mentally transpose the environment he sees on the screen to the stage where he is acting. No simple trick.

But despite the difficulties, actors are working in this new medium. The CD-ROM game *Return To Zork*, boasts a cast of twenty-three actors. Some stars are even working with the new technology. The CD-ROM interactive movie called *Under A Killing Moon*, features such well-known film actors as Brian Keith, Margot Kidder and Russell Means. Multimedia has become important enough that super agency ICM (International Creative Management) has developed an interactive wing. Former Apple Computer Chairman John Scully predicts that interactive media will become a 3 *trillion* dollar business within the next decade. For the actor, this new venue will mean more work. The real question, though, is whether audiences really *want* to interact with the stories they are told, or whether they want to sit back and let the storyteller do the work.

Another technology that offers increased opportunities for the actor is cable television. Although the promise of 500 channels is somewhat overstated, 200 or 300 channels does seem possible in the near future. Many of these channels will be special interest types and will not feature actors. But many will be entertainment outlets, needing performers. The catch may be, though, that the greater quantity of work made available by these additional channels will result in smaller salaries for each individual project.

These new digital technologies are certainly stunning. They present the pleasing promise of unlimited control, dressed in slick interfaces and smooth operating systems. But during our infatuation with them, it seems that only the shiniest surfaces capture our attention. Where, one wonders, do *humans* fit into all of this?

The actor of today and tomorrow is faced with the possibility of being replaced, being sampled, and acting in the vacuum of an ultimatte set, with a dazzling variety of unseen special effects. Why act at all if this is the reality? If the actor is to be removed from his fellow actors, from his surroundings, and even separated from his voice and body image by the new technology, what reward is there for him? Why do it?

Since the dawn of time, people have enacted their stories in only an empty space, the spectators and actors using only their imaginations to "see" the props, the ghosts, the armies, the palaces. Mankind's urge to talk to itself, to participate in a grand collective dream, is fundamental and universal. With or without technology, this need will find expression. Children hear a story and declare, "I'm the princess." Their identification, total. Adults watch a movie and are moved to tears or laughter. Their empathy, complete. This enlivening of both the imagination and the emotions is one of the cherished purposes of art. It is why we seek it out. As a celebration of the mind, the imagination and the emotions, art has a unique power to make us all feel more human. The actor has a special role to play in this.

Every character has a right to have its story told. Without an actor, this character floats in space, mute and unseen. The actor's role is to serve as an honest and passionate advocate for this one, unique point of view. No matter what form the story takes – play, film, television, video game or interactive CD – the actor must keep his focus. The future may be uncertain, but his purpose is not. No matter what technology of recording or projection is used, the actor's job is to give passionate form to character, and to illuminate the human soul in all its glorious complexity. In the end, technology should serve the imagination, and not enslave it.

The future remains to be seen.

AFTERWORD

As the director steps out of the movie house and into the night, he reflects on what he has seen. Flat people on a flat screen had moved him. Why? Why did this celluloid succeed, and his experiment in the theater fail? These questions gnaw at him as he makes his way down the street. He must have an answer. His creative imagination begins to waken as he finds himself in front of an all night camera store. In the window is an antiquated Super 8 film camera. He stares at it, as if hypnotized. Visions dizzy his brain. A moment later, he disappears into the shop.

APPENDIX

The Bomb Exercise

An exercise designed to show how having a compelling *action* to play frees the actor from both camera and self-consciousness.

An object is presented to the actor as a very powerful and highly unstable bomb. (The object used for this "bomb" should consist of three or four interlocking parts that can be unfastened. I find that a coffee cup holder designed for attachment to car windows is a particularly useful device for this exercise.)

The bomb is placed on a flat or tilted surface. The actor is told that he or she must disarm this bomb, by breaking it down into its component parts. The bomb is sensitive to vibration, and if it "senses" that it is being moved, it will go off. So, the actor must move it extremely slowly and precisely. The bomb is sensitive to moisture changes in the air, so that the actor must be careful not to breathe on it, or it will explode. Since the bomb is sensitive to moisture, the actor's hands must be dry, and not sweaty. Further, the bomb is sensitive to the movement of the air surrounding it, so the actor must approach it with tremendous care, or it will detonate. Many other circumstances can be added. The actor is shown *one* time how to take the "bomb" apart. Then it is up to him. If the actor succeeds in doing this, he has survived. If not, he is dead.

This exercise is done with a video tape camera rolling.

As the actor enters into the reality of the circumstance, he becomes so totally involved in disarming the bomb without setting it off that he loses all awareness of the camera. The camera can even be moved in order to shoot from different angles, and the actor will not later be able to recall where the camera was, or if it moved at all. The actor also forgets to "control" his face, so that very realistic and unclichéd behavior results.

This exercise is an intense one for the participants, and the tension of the scene can be felt even in the video playback. After experiencing and seeing this exercise, remind the actor that if he can bring the same concentration and commitment to the roles he plays, he will be able to enter into them fully and believably. If an actor feels himself dropping out of a scene, he must remind himself that the bomb is ticking away.

CRITICAL BIBLIOGRAPHY

Film Background

Barnouw, Erik, *Tube of Plenty* .
Oxford University Press, New York, 1990.
A revelatory history of the evolution of American radio and television. Well written and full of surprising information.

Cook, David, *A History Of Narrative Film.*
W.W. Norton & Co., New York, 1990.
One of the finest single volume film histories available. Includes an excellent discussion of the development of the Classic Hollywood style, and is written in a scholarly but highly accessible style.

Katz, Steven D., *Film Directing Shot By Shot.*
Wiese Production, Calif., 1991.
Even though aimed primarily at directors, this book provides the actor with clear explanations of the 180° rule and how to violate it, directorial processes including story boarding, and how to think visually. An excellent book.

Miller, Mark Crispin, editor, *Seeing Through Movies.*
Pantheon Books, New York, 1990.
Six interesting and sometimes provocative essays by thoughtful film critics, and film studies professors. Fine examinations of the "Blockbuster," movies as advertising, and Hollywood's treatment of the Vietnam war. Very stimulating.

Robertson, Joseph, *The Magic of Film Editing.*
Tab Books Inc., Pennsylvania, 1983.
This book provides the actor with a simple but clear explanation of the editing process, providing a perspective the actor usually lacks.

Seger and Whetmore, *From Script to Screen.*
Henry Holt & Co., New York, 1994.
The best single volume overview of the film process available. This book covers the pre-production, production and post-production phases through interviews and comments from filmmakers themselves. As few books do,

this one makes powerfully clear the collaborative nature of filmmaking. Writers, producers, directors, actors, editors, production designers, and effects co-ordinators are all included. Especially valuable are discussions of the auditioning process, and of the shooting process as it pertains to actors. A superb book.

Silver, A., Ward, E., *The Film Director's Team.*
Silman-James Press, L.A., 1992.
A good look at who does what during the three phases of production. Excellent examples of production boards and call sheets.

Acting For the Camera

Abbott, Leslie, *Acting for Films and TV.*
Star Publishing Co., 1994.
This book provides good exercises and some sound advice. Particularly valuable for the scenes included.

Adams, Brian, *Screen Acting.*
Lone Eagle Publishing Co., 1986-7.
A somewhat scattered approach to the subject featuring some good comments from well known actors, but without any context. Adequate coverage of topics.

Barr, Tony, *Acting for the Camera.*
Allyn & Bacon, Inc., Boston, 1982.
For many years, one of the only valuable texts on the subject. This book is still a sound guide to the basic problems of camera acting. Barr offers good practical advice in a clear and concise style.

Bernard, Ian, *Film And Television Acting.*
Focal Press, 1993.
Some good practical advice and exercises give this book its value.

Butler, Jeremy G., editor, *Star Texts.*
Wayne State University Press, Detroit, 1991.
A compilation of articles by Stanislavsky, Pudovkin, Kuleshov, Strasberg, Brecht and Bresson that contain many useful ideas. The rest of the book contains articles by academics and critics on semiology, particular stars, and television.

Bibliography

Caine, Michael, *Acting in Film*.
Applause Theater Book Publishers, 1990.
Good information from a fine film acting professional. Caine offers some excellent practical tips on close-ups, preparation, working with directors and fellow actors, and offers many important insights into the dynamics of a working set. A very good book.

Kuleshov, Lev, (Dmitri Agrachev, translator), *Fifty Years in Film*.
Raduga Publishers, Moscow, 1987.
A collection of essays, articles and speeches by Kuleshov. Especially interesting is a section on Kuleshov's experimental film workshop and his training syllabus for film actors.

Naremore, James, *Acting In The Cinema*.
University of California Press, Berkeley, 1988.
A fascinating look at how actors communicate meaning. This book applies the literary theories of semiotics to acting. And while actors will find little of practical usefulness in this approach, it affords a rare look at how the academic community grapples with the nature of acting.

O'Brien, Mary Ellen, *Film Acting*.
Arco Publishing, Inc, 1983.
One of the very best books on the subject. Not only does it contain good practical advice, but it also places film acting in some historical perspective. An excellent book.

Pudovkin, V.I., *Film Technique And Film Acting*.
Grove Press, Inc., 1958, 1976.
Although *Film Acting* was written in 1949, it remains the single most important document on the subject. As no other book does, Pudovkin's integrates theoretical speculation with practical reality. His grasp of the entire film process is equaled only by his ability to communicate it to others. A seminal work.

Tucker, Patrick, *Secrets of Screen Acting*.
Rutledge Press, New York, 1994.
Despite a British viewpoint that accepts a bit more theatricality than some Americans might like, this book provides an excellent examination of the subject. Tucker is insightful about adjusting performance size to shot size, and includes a good discussion of performing within frames. This thoughtful book also offers many interesting exercises.

General Acting

Adler, Stella, *The Technique of Acting*.
Bantam Books, New York, 1988.
A superb book from one of the only American teachers to have worked with Stanislavsky. Her break with Strasberg over the importance of emotion memory lead her to develop a view of acting closer perhaps to Stanislavsky's. Excellent exercises round out this fine offering.

Benedetti, Jean, *Stanislavsky*.
Routledge, New York, 1988.
The best and most up to date biography of Stanislavsky available in English. Benedetti has included new material only available since the advent of *Glasnost*. Stanislavsky's theories and the forces that shaped them are examined with clarity and thoughtfulness. A real achievement.

Benedetti, Robert L., *Seeming, Being and Becoming*.
Drama Book Specialists, New York, 1976.
This book not only places the development of twentieth century acting in historical perspective, but offers a unique final section containing a personal philosophy of drama and performance.

Boleslavsky, Richard, *Acting: The First Six Lessons*.
Theater Arts Books, New York, 1933, 1991.
A standard in the field. Boleslavsky was an actor in Stanislavsky's theater. After touring the U.S., he decided to remain and teach. Co-founder of the American Laboratory Theater, he was Strasberg's teacher, among others. This book is a classic. Engagingly written and profound.

Bruder, Melissa, et al, *A Practical Handbook For the Actor*.
Vintage Books, New York, 1986.
A distillation of acting methods based on Stanislavsky, as filtered through the teachings of playwright David Mamet. A no-nonsense guide to some of the most important craft questions that face the actor. Clear and concise.

Callow, Simon, *Being An Actor*.
Grove Press, 1984.
A first hand account of the life of a stage actor from unemployment to the end of a run. Well written and insightful.

Bibliography

Clurman, Harold, *The Fervent Years*.
Da Capo Press, 1945, 1975.
This great director and teacher's account of the history and methods of the Group Theater is an exhilarating experience. Clurman's vivid writing and astute insights bring this exciting period of discovery to life. A book that communicates not just the facts of the theater, but its heart and soul.

Hagen, Uta, *A Challenge for the Actor*.
MacMillan Publishing Co., New York, 1991.
A useful book that is part instructional and part memoir. The exercises are particularly good. Excellent for the more advanced actor.

Hagen, Uta, *Respect for Acting*.
MacMillan Publishing Co., New York, 1973.
An excellent book. This fine actress and teacher's discussion of substitution and emotional and sense memory are particularly fine. She also provides some excellent exercises.

Hethman, Robert H., editor, *Strasberg at the Actor's Studio*.
Theater Communications Group, New York, 1965, 1991.
This book is unique in that it contains transcriptions of some of Lee Strasberg's private teaching sessions. A good example of this important teacher at work.

Hirsch, Foster, *A Method To Their Madness*.
W.W. Norton and Company, Inc., New York, 1984.
A look at the history and practice of the Actor's Studio. Includes comments by Strasberg, Elia Kazan, and Arthur Penn. Fascinating.

Hull, Lorrie, *Strasberg's Method*.
Ox Bow Publishing, Inc., 1985.
The most comprehensive of the books available on the Method. Hull, a leading teacher at the Studio, guides the reader through the most important exercises developed by Strasberg and others. Provides the most detailed look at the actual curriculum of the Actor's Studio.

Johnstone, Keith, *Impro*.
Routledge Press, New York, 1981-1987, 1987.
A great complement to Viola Spolin's book, cited on the next page. Johnstone is particularly good in his examination of status as an improvisational tool.

Manderino, Ned, *All About Method Acting*.
Manderino Books, Calif., 1985.
A straightforward presentation of some of the central exercises taught at the Actor's Studio. Also includes some good exercises of Manderino's own devising.

Meisner, Sanford, *On Acting*.
Random House, Inc., New York, 1987.
Member of the Group Theater, founder of the Neighborhood Playhouse in New York, and master teacher, Meisner has written an excellent book featuring actual working sessions with students. An interesting alternative to Strasberg.

Miller, Alan, *A Passion For Acting*.
Backstage Books, New York, 1992.
A clear and honest account of Miller's own training at the Actor's Studio. Contains some of the most useful thoughts on the process of acting in print. Well written, with some pointed anecdotes.

Smith, Wendy, *Real Life Drama*.
Grove Weidenfeld, 1990.
A history of the Group Theater from 1931-1940. Includes some of the central figures of the American theater: Harold Clurman, Elia Kazan, Lee Strasberg, Stella Adler, Sanford Meisner, Clifford Odets, Robert Lewis, Cheryl Crawford and Morris Carnovsky.

Spolin, Viola, *Improvisation for the Theater*.
Northwestern University Press, 1983.
This book created improvisational theater as we know it today. Spolin devised a series of what she called Theater Games originally for children. In the fifties, Compass Theater in Chicago began to use these games as the basis for improvisational theater. Members of this troupe included Mike Nichols and Elaine May. Compass Theater soon evolved into the famous Second City of Chicago. Her son, Paul Sills, went on to use her techniques to create Story Theater. This book contains most of the important games that became the basis for improvisational theater around the world.

Stanislavsky, Constantine, *An Actor Prepares, Creating a Role, Building a Character*.
Theater Arts Books, New York, 1948, 1961.
The best and most influential books on acting ever written. To get the full thrust of Stanislavsky's ideas and evolution, all three books must be read.

Bibliography

New translations are forthcoming from Jean Benedetti which will include much more material than the standard texts. Seminal works.

Strasberg, Lee, *A Dream of Passion*.
Little, Brown and Company, Boston, 1987.
More a memoir than a book on technique. It provides an interesting glimpse into this influential teacher's motivations and thoughts. Not the grand summation of the Method that some may have hoped for, but perhaps all the better for that. A "definitive" book might have petrified Strasberg's work. An interesting discussion of Brecht and the Method.

Other Acting Books of Interest

Bates, Brian, *The Way of the Actor*.
Shambhala Publications, Inc., Boston, 1987.

Cohen, Robert, *Acting One*.
Mayfield Publishing, 1992.

Cohen, Robert, *Acting Power*.
Mayfield Publishing, 1978.

Morris, Eric, Hotchkiss, Joan, *No Acting Please*.
Spelling Publications, Los Angeles, 1977, 1979.

Suzuki, T., *The Way of Acting*.
Theater Communications Group, 1986.

GLOSSARY

Abby Singer
The shot before the last shot of the day. Named in honor of former first A.D., Abby Singer, who used to call the last shot of the day one shot too early.

Action
What a character *does* in support of an objective. For example, if a character's objective is "to leave," a supporting action might be *to pack.* If a character does an action *not* in support of the objective, that is a clue to the character's inner thoughts. For example, if a character says they want to leave but stops packing, then it might be that the character really wishes to stay.

"Action!"
The command from the director for the scene to begin.
Actors should not wait for "action" to begin acting. They should begin a few moments before, so that they are already "in" the scene as action is said.

A.D.R.
Automated Dialogue Replacement. See *looping.*

Best Boy
The assistant to the Chief Electrician, or Head Gaffer.

Blocking
The movements of the actors or the camera.

Blue Screen
Shooting in a studio against a large blue or greenish backdrop, allows a background to later be superimposed on the final image. The actors must imagine the set they are on and be aware of the limitations of their movements.
Many CD-ROM video games using actors are shot on blue screen sound stages. The actor has the problem of staying within lines that they don't see.

Boom Operator
The member of the sound department responsible for holding the boom pole, with mic attached, over and sometimes under, the actors. Also

Glossary

responsible for placing radio mics on actors.
Working closely with the boom operator and the sound mixer can help an actor to avoid looping.

Call Sheet
A sheet containing the cast and crew call times for a specific day's shooting. Scene numbers, the expected day's total pages, locations, and production needs are also included.
Each actor has a number, assigned to him by the U.P.M. An actor should look for his cast number across from the scene listed, to determine if he is in that particular scene.

Camera Crew
With the D.P. as its chief, this team consists of the camera operator, the first assistant camera operator (focus puller), the second assistant camera operator (film loader and clapstick clapper) and the dolly grip.

Camera Left
Left, from the camera's point of view. Opposite of stage left, which is the actor's point of view as he faces the audience. If the actor is facing the camera, camera left is the actor's right.

Camera Operator
The member of the camera crew who actually looks through the lens during a take. Responsible for panning and tilting and keeping the action within the frame.
If an actor is concerned about leaning or walking out of frame, asking the camera operator for help is appropriate. Asking the D.P. is not.

Camera Right
Right, from the camera's point of view. Opposite of stage right, which is the actor's point of view as she faces the audience. If the actor is facing the camera, camera right is the actor's left.

Caterer
Responsible for breakfast, lunch and dinner on a set. Different from *craft services.*

CD-ROM
A compact disk that holds text, music and images. One of the principal new venues for interactive video games as well as for full motion video films.
Acting for CD-ROM's is a new arena for actors. The Screen Actor's Guild and

AFTRA both have contracts covering salaries and working conditions in this new medium. Check with these unions when working with this technology.

Cheat

Because distances and locations look different to the camera than they do in real life, an actor might be asked to look at a different place than where the other actor actually is. On camera it looks fine, but to the actor it is a cheat. For example, an actor might be asked to cheat a look or a body position more toward the camera than the actor would think necessary or even comfortable. But to the camera, such a cheat would look perfectly natural.

Cinematographer

See Director of Photography.

Classic Hollywood Style

A style of filmmaking emphasizing the continuous flow of action. Designed to hide from audience perception the fact that films are composed of many small pieces of film, edited together. Also refers to the process of shooting a *master*, a *two-shot*, matching *over-the-shoulders*, and matching *close-ups*.

Close-up (C.U.)

A camera shot showing the head and sometimes the upper chest of a character. The close-up carries the emotional expression of the actor best of all the shots, because it is such an intimate one.

Coverage

All shots *other* than the master. (*Two-shot, over-the-shoulder, close-up.*)

Craft Services

The snack cart on a set. It usually has water, coffee, dough-nuts, cereal, milk and various kinds of junk food. Stick as much as possible with the fruits and vegetables, however. Does not supply breakfast, lunch or dinner, but is always available.

Cut

On the set, "cut" is a command from the director to stop the shooting, acting and sound recording. The only people other than the director who can stop the action are the *camera operator* and the *mixer*.
An actor can, at NO time, call a cut. No matter what happens, the actor keeps acting and stays in the scene until he hears "cut."
Directors do not always call cut when the dialogue is finished. Sometimes they let the camera roll in the hopes of capturing some spontaneous bit of behavior or

improvised dialogue that will be usable. This is possible only if the actor stays committed to the scene even after he thinks it is over.

Dailies
The previous day's shooting after the film has been processed and is ready for viewing. Dailies often are screened at lunch time and if actors want to see them they should ask the director for permission.

Many producers and directors do not want actors at the dailies because they feel they cannot talk freely about what they are seeing. They are also afraid that the actor will become self-conscious and either like himself too much or dislike himself too much and then change what he's been doing on the next day of shooting. On the other hand, actors can learn a great deal about what works on camera and what doesn't by attending dailies. But actors should do so only if their ego is secure and can watch them as objectively as possible.

Day Out of Days
A schedule of shooting showing what scenes will be shot on what days.

An actor with a part stretching over many days will find a copy of a day out of days invaluable. But remember that this schedule is subject to constant revision, so keep it current by asking the 2nd A.D. for an updated copy.

Dolly
The wheeled platform to which the camera is attached, making possible *tracking* shots.

Dolly Grip
The grip who moves the dolly. A vital part of the camera crew.

Dubbing
The re-recording of dialogue into another language. This is different from *looping.*

Double System
The fact that in film the *image* is recorded onto the film in the camera but that the *dialogue* is recorded onto tape into a separate tape recorder.

Director of Photography (D.P.)
Also known as the *D.P.* The D.P. is responsible for the look of the film. He is in charge of the lighting, the color tones, the film stock, the lenses, chooses the processing lab, and helps the director decide on the camera angles. He is the crew chief of the camera crew.

He or she is usually one of the people holding a light meter to the actor's forehead. There is no reason for the actor to bother this person with questions.

Electricians
The people who adjust, focus, gel, filter and maneuver the lights. Their crew chief is the *Gaffer* or Chief Electrician.

First A.D.
First Assistant Director. The 1st A.D. runs the set. If he calls for crews to stop working, they stop working. When the camera is ready he calls for the first team. He calls for quiet on the set, calls for rehearsal if that's what the director wants, and calls for the camera and sound to roll. He directs the extras and helps prepare each day's call sheet.

First Asst. Cam. Op.
First Assistant Camera Operator. This member of the camera crew adjusts the focus of the lens during the shooting of a scene. For this reason, he is known also as the *focus puller.*
When an actor is on her mark, the focus puller will be measuring the precise distance of that actor to the focal plane of the lens. This is done with a tape measure, one end of which is attached to the camera, and one end of which the focus puller brings to the actor's face. The focus puller then notes the best setting for a clear focus on a small note pad which is also attached to the camera. If an actor leans in or away from the lens during the scene, the focus puller will also measure THAT distance for a correct focal setting. If a focus puller asks an actor to show him her lean, the actor must do it as she would in performance so that his measurements will be accurate when the camera rolls.

First Positions
See *Number One.*

First Team
The principal actors in a particular scene.

Focus Puller
See *First Assistant Camera Operator.*

Gaffer
The Chief Electrician, or Head Gaffer. This person is the crew chief of the electricians who work the lighting instruments. Works closely with the Director of Photography.
This person is usually known to the actor as one of the people who holds a light

Glossary

meter to his head. the other person who does this is the Director of Photography.

Grips
A large crew of people responsible for moving set furniture, light poles, laying dolly track, and doing work that requires physical labor.
If an actor moves a chair out of place during the playing of a scene, he should let a grip place it back on its mark if another take is required. That is their job.

Hold
An indication on a call sheet that an actor will probably not be working on that given day.

Key Light
The strongest light source in a scene.

Kuleshov Effect
Named for the Russian filmmaker and teacher Lev Kuleshov who articulated the idea that the emotional meaning of an expression on an actor's face is determined by the shots surrounding it. An actor's neutral expression will be read by the audience as sorrow if the image following it is of a person lying in a coffin, or as joy, if the image following it is a child at play.

Line of Action
Also known as the *line of axis*, or simply the *line*. See *180° Rule*.

Line Objective
What a character *wants* with each line they say. If a character asks a question, the line objective is to get an answer. Adding up the line objectives helps the actor to determine the character's *scene objective*. Always phrased as an action (verb) statement.

Line Producer
The producer responsible for keeping the director on time and on budget. Of the various producers, it is the line producer who is most often on the set.

Looping
The process of re-recording dialogue in a sound studio. This is done for a variety of reasons:
1) The *production track* is not clean due to poor recording, 2) environmental noise makes the dialogue unclear such as an airplane overhead, 3) a

producer or director wishes to add new dialogue to a scene, 4) a producer or director wants to alter the actor's performance in some way, or 5) the actor must match another actor's loops so that the dialogue and background sound are even.

Actors are often surprised how much of their performance must be looped. It is useful to understand that most dialogue recorded outside (exterior) will probably have to be looped.

If a scene is a particularly challenging one, the actor can ask the mixer what he can do to help the recording process so that he will not be forced to loop the scene weeks or months later.

Marks

Positions given to the camera, the actor and the objects to be photographed, so that they are in focus and in the proper light.

Actors' marks are put down either with gaffer's tape or with chalk. Just before the camera rolls, the marks are removed.

Matching Actions

The fact that actors must match their physical movements from shot to shot so that they can create the illusion of a continuous performance. If an actor picks up a glass with her left hand in the master, she must pick it up with the same hand in the two-shot, the over and the close-up. Small movements or shifts do *not* need to be matched exactly because the viewer cannot remember every tiny motion. But if major actions are not matched, the actor may find some of his work on the cutting room floor.

Master Shot

A shot far enough away to hold most of the actor's body, but close enough so that the characters are recognizable. The goal of this shot is to record the scene from beginning to end. In continuity shooting, the master serves as the reference shot into which footage from the other angles will be inserted. The master also gives a sense of context to the scene because it includes a good portion of the background.

Mixer

The senior member of the sound crew. This person works at a sound cart with a mixer and tape recorder and is responsible for the quality of the sound.

Morphing

The digital manipulation of objects or an actor's body so that it can be seamlessly transformed into some other shape. Done as a special effect in post-production.

Glossary

MOS
A scene without sound in it when it is shot. Sound will likely be added later in post-production. For example, a person searching someone's hotel room would most likely be shot MOS. Such a scene may be a long one, including some coverage, but calls for no dialogue. Later, appropriate sounds and music may be added. The story goes that the term comes either from a German or Hungarian film director working in Hollywood who called for a shot "*Mitt Out Sound.*"

Number One
The command usually given by the 1st A.D. for the actors and the camera to go back to their first positions for the beginning of the shot.

Obstacle
That which prevents the character from attaining his objective. If the objective is to steal someone's wife away, the obstacle is the husband (and maybe the wife).

180° Rule
The fact that the camera can be placed anywhere along an imaginary 180° line drawn through the heads of the actors in a scene. If the camera crosses this line when shooting coverage, screen direction will be askew. This rule can be violated, but is generally observed especially when shooting by cuts (no moving camera).

One-Liner
A schedule of what scenes will be shot on what days. A one-liner is less complete than a *day out of days,* but is useful to an actor for preparation if a day out of days is not available.
An actor can get a one-liner from a second A.D.

Overlapping
This term refers to two or more people talking at once.
In a close-up, actors should not overlap dialogue even if they have done so in all previous shots, unless specifically told to do so by the director. One reason for this is that sound editors like to have clean tracks of each character's dialogue so they have more control over the final mix.

Over-the-shoulder (O.T.S.)
In this shot, the camera is placed behind one actor's shoulder so that a part of that actor's body takes up a corner of the frame. The rest of the frame is

taken up with the face, or the chest and face, of the other actor in the scene. It is an intimate shot and can record a great deal of emotional expression from the actor on whom the camera is focused. Overs are almost always shot in matching pairs, so that the expressions and reactions of each actor can be seen.

Pan
The side to side (left to right or vice versa) movement of the camera.
In order for the operator to follow an actor, the actor usually needs to move a little slower than he would in real life. If a quick motion is necessary, the actor must make sure that the operator knows about it.

Persistence of Vision
The name given by Peter Mark Roget in 1824 to the physiological fact that an image stays on the brain for 1/5th to 1/20th of a second after that image has been removed from the field of view. This fact allows us to view a rapidly moving series of still pictures as continuous motion.

Personalization
The first level of the actor's process. Personalizing material means exploring one's personal responses to the text and to one's fellow actor. It is a time when the actor is not obligated to fulfill the demands of the material but rather is allowed to follow his own impulses and honest reactions whether or not they seem appropriate to the author's intentions. At the personalization level, the actor crosses out all stage directions including emotional directions such as "she laughs," or "he cries" and explores *his* reactions. In this way, the actor often finds a non-clichéd approach to his role.

Plot Objective
What the character wants over the course of the entire play or screenplay. Always stated as an action phrase. For example, "I want to escape."

P.O.V. (Point of View)
A script indication showing the viewpoint of a character. The camera itself becomes the eyes of that character.

Post-production
The phase of the filmmaking process that begins after footage has been shot. This includes sound and picture editing, titling, dubbing, negative cutting and releasing a final print.

Glossary

Pre-production
The phase of filmmaking that begins before any film has been shot. This includes rewriting the script, scouting locations, hiring crews, casting major parts, creating a shooting schedule, and ordering equipment.

Print
On the set, a command from the director that a particular take is good enough to be printed up for the dailies.

Production
The actual shooting phase of the filmmaking process.

Production Company
The company actually making the film or television show. Most projects are made by independent production companies who sell the distribution rights to a major studio, network or cable company.

Production Track
The sound obtained during the actual shooting.

Prop Department
The crew chief of this department is the *Prop Master*. Responsible for all props as well as special effects.

Room Tone
Also known as *presence* or *ambiance*. The sound of the shooting location when it is quiet.
When the 1st A.D. announces that room tone is about to be recorded, actors and everyone else should stop talking or moving. Usually about two minutes of ambiance is recorded.

Scene Objective
What a character wants during any particular scene. The objective should always be phrased as a simple action (verb) statement.

Script Supervisor
The person on a set who records how long each take of a scene is, who is on and off camera in every take, which takes are printed, what went wrong with the ones that weren't printed, records the movements of the actors to make sure they are consistent, and helps the actors with their lines. A copy of her notes is given to the editor at the end of each day's shooting.
Actors should NOT rely on the script supervisor to keep their continuity straight.

These people simply have too much to do to notice and record every single thing an actor does. The actor himself must be responsible for remembering where he was and what he did.

Second A.D.
2nd Assistant Director. Usually there are two or three seconds on a set. They are the people an actor checks in with when she arrives on a set. They are responsible for getting the actors their contracts, tax and immigration forms, and script revisions. If an actor needs something, it is best to ask a second A.D. for it first.
Never leave a set without checking first with a 2nd A.D. At the end of each day's work, the 2nd A.D. must sign an actor out.

Second Asst. Cam. Op.
Second Assistant Camera Operator. This member of the camera crew operates the clapsticks and unloads the film after it has been shot.

Second Team
The stand-ins for the principle actors.
After the action of a scene has been rehearsed for the camera, the main actors are allowed to leave the set for make-up touch-up or to go over lines, or to rest while the crew lights the scene with the stand-ins.

Set-up
Every time the camera changes position it is a new set-up.

Spiking the Lens
Looking straight into the camera lens during a scene. Actors do not spike the lens because it destroys the audience's sense of invisibility.
Never look directly into the lens during a scene unless specifically directed to do so.

Stand-ins
See *Second Team.*

Strategy
The way a character tries to overcome an obstacle in order to attain an objective. If a character wants to borrow money from a friend (the objective), the friend is reluctant (the obstacle), the character might try to flatter the friend in order to get the money (a strategy), threaten the friend in order to get it (another strategy), beg the friend (yet another strategy), or use guilt to get the money (still another strategy). Using different strategies in a scene can give it a variety and texture and keep a performance from becoming monotonous.

Glossary

Stunt Double
A stunt person who does a stunt for a principal actor.

SW
An indication on a call sheet that an actor is *Starting* on that day, and *Working* on that day.

SWF
An indication on a call sheet that an actor is *Starting* on that day, *Working* on that day and will be *Finished* working on the project that very same day.

Sync Lines
On-screen dialogue lines where the movement of the mouth is clearly seen. Looping sync lines means matching the movement of the lips very precisely.

Take
Each roll of the camera from a particular setup. In the master, for instance, the first roll of the camera is the first *take*, the second roll of the camera is the *second take*, and so on.

Tilt
The up and down movement of the camera.
In order for the operator to follow an actor sitting or rising, the actor needs to move a little more slowly than they would in real life. If a fast move is necessary, make sure the operator knows about it.

Tracking Shot
A shot wherein the camera is moving, either on tracks that have been laid down or on a vehicle.

Two-shot
Closer than a master, this shot brings the viewer nearer to the actors. Both actors can be clearly seen but not full body.

Typage
The idea, formulated by Kuleshov and used by Sergei Eisenstein, that real people should be used to act in films and not actors. Abandoned in the late thirties in favor of actors trained to deal with the special demands of camera acting.

U.P.M.
The Unit Production Manager. Oversees the crews, is responsible for

scheduling, and for the technical requirements of the production. Prepares and approves the *call sheet.*

V.O. (Voice Over)
An off-camera voice coming from either a machine such as an intercom or telephone, or a character not yet in frame.

W
An indication on a call sheet that an actor is *Working* on that day.

Wardrobe Department (Costumer)
After an actor gets a job, the first people to contact her will be from this department. They will want an actor's sizes, so know them. They will also want to schedule a fitting appointment. An actor's costume is an important part of her characterization, so give serious thought to this part of your job; the costumer will have.

An actor can also, by discreet questioning, find out many important things from the costumer. She can ask what days her character is working, what the locations will be, if the production is behind or on schedule, what the feeling on the set is, and so on. Knowing what's ahead gives the actor precious lead time for preparation.

Wild Track
Any non-sync dialogue.

W/N
Means *Will Notify.* An indication on a call sheet that means the actor will probably work that day, but no specific time has yet been decided on.

Wrap
The last shot of the day, or of the whole project, or of a particular actor's work on a project.

INDEX

Index

Index

The Camera Smart Actor